$\mathcal{LO}$

THIS BOOK IS A MUST-READ for all of us for one simple reason: All of us are addicts, and we cannot break our addictions alone. Whether our attachments are to a substance or a relationship; to comfort, competition, security or praise, we are not fully alive while under their control. *Loving an Addict* is not a book of platitudes or easy answers, thank God, but a lively and honest companion into and through the pain of addiction. The author's hard won wisdom, together with the wisdom of scripture, helps us to see the universal truth that the addict is not "out there" but "in here." We can learn to love all parts of ourselves. We can become more fully the people God longs for us to be.

—KAYLA MCCLURG
inward/outward, an online project of
The Church of the Saviour, Washington, DC

NO SPIRITUAL PRACTICE HAS HELPED me more on my journey with God than keeping company with Jesus in the Gospels. By sharing honestly her experiences of this practice, against the challenging backdrop of learning to love her husband in spiritually healthier ways as he battled alcoholism, Alyssa Phillips both encourages and guides us in praying the Gospels. This book will help all of us seeking to live faithfully when faced with challenges in intimate relationships.

—Trevor Hudson
Author of *A Mile in My Shoes: Cultivating Compassion*
and *One Day at a Time: Discovering the Freedom
of 12-Step Spirituality*

ALYSSA PHILLIPS WRITES a deeply moving account of her journey with a loved one who suffers from addiction issues. For those who believe in Christ, this is a very important book, particularly in Phillips's use of scripture as a resource to strengthen and guide her along this difficult path.

—Alan R. Burt
Author of *Blessings of the Burden: Reflections and
Lessons in Helping the Homeless*

ALYSSA PHILLIPS

LOVING AN ADDICT

GOSPEL REFLECTIONS OF HOPE AND HEALING

UPPER ROOM BOOKS®
NASHVILLE

LIBRARY OF CONGRESS CATALOGING-IN-PUBLICATION DATA

ISBN 978-0-8358-1369-3 (print)—ISBN 978-0-8358-1370-9(mobi)—ISBN 978-0-8358-1371-6 (epub)

Printed in the United States of America

For my dear friend

Eartha,

whose faithful and loving heart
always inspires

Contents

	Preface	9
	Introduction	13
1	When Our Words Become Flesh	17
2	Turning toward the Light	20
3	Clinging to God's Promises	23
4	From Pride to Vulnerability	26
5	The Treasure of Memories	29
6	The Challenge of Obedience	32
7	The "Wild Beasts" of Temptation	35
8	Discerning God's Authentic Call	38
9	Feeding on God's Word	41
10	When We Can't Seem to Grow	44
11	Radical Acceptance and Radical Challenge	47
12	Embracing Repentance	50
13	When Despair Overwhelms Us	53
14	Repenting, Believing, and Following	56
15	From Depletion to Restoration	59
16	How Do We Need to Be Healed?	62
17	Objectivity and Compassion	65
18	Purity, the Core of Righteousness	68
19	When We Struggle in Prayer	71
20	Self-Awareness and Obedience to the Lord	74
21	Bringing Our Burdens to Jesus	77
22	The Gift of a Spiritual Family	79
23	Tilling the Soil of Our Hearts	82
24	Faith in the Midst of the Storm	85
25	When Wisdom Meets Innocence	88

26	Crying Out for Help	91
27	The Gift of an Eternal Perspective	94
28	The Blessing of Jesus' Humanity	97
29	Pain as the Training Ground for Discipleship	100
30	Listening to the Lord	103
31	The Courage to Surrender in Prayer	106
32	Forgiveness and the Heart of Prayer	109
33	Our Loved Ones as Neighbors	112
34	Sitting at Jesus' Feet	115
35	Radical Grace in God's Kingdom	118
36	What Does Jesus Mean by Hate?	121
37	The Elder Brother in Our Hearts	124
38	The Comfort of Jesus' Tears	127
39	The Paradox of Peace	130
40	The Challenge of a Biblical Anger	133
41	Codependency vs. Surrender to the Lord	136
42	Marriage and the Kingdom of Heaven	139
43	Readiness, Responsibility, and Recognition	142
44	Obeying God's Nudges in Our Hearts	145
45	Resources for Radical Love	148
46	The Temptation Not to Pray	151
47	Daring to Draw Closer to the Cross	154
48	The Agony of Abandonment	157
49	Jesus' Victory and Our Ultimate Hope	160
50	Glimpses of a Larger Reality	163
51	Believing What We Have Not Yet Seen	166
52	The Promise of Jesus' Eternal Presence	169
	Bibliography	173
	About the Author	175

Preface

Resources abound for addicted men and women, but books for those of us who love them are fewer and farther between. Yet we too have struggles.

I speak from personal experience. I knew during our engagement that Carl, my husband-to-be, had a long-standing problem with alcohol. I brought to our relationship my difficulty in dealing with anger. We loved each other though and believed God wanted us to marry. Each of us had suffered the pain of divorce, so we set ourselves the task of doing better the second time around.

Of course we faced challenges. For me, these came to a head one night at an ocean-front motel where we'd gone to escape the stresses piling up at home. There in that tiny bedroom, my husband started drinking. Soon the alcohol began to take its toll on us both. Desperate to get away, I sought refuge in the bathroom, closing the lid of the toilet seat and turning it into a makeshift chair, where I sat in utter misery.

I had a Bible and my journal. Sitting there I began to browse in the Gospel of John, pausing at the passage in chapter 2 that describes Jesus' cleansing of the Temple. That picture of Jesus' fury riveted me. Grabbing my journal, I began to write frantically. It all came out: my anger at my husband and at the terrible demon of addiction, coupled with shame over how I had lost my temper in a painful emotional meltdown. As I wrote, I could sense the Holy Spirit's presence; eventually my anger and shame calmed, and repentance softened my heart.

I had been attending Al-Anon, the Alcoholics Anonymous-related fellowship for families and friends of alcoholics, since early in our marriage (though what I share in these pages reflects my own perspective rather than that of any particular recovery movement). Al-Anon provided help in many ways, but those meetings never facilitated the kind of healing I experienced that night through scripture. As I continued journaling with the Gospels over the next few months, I realized that this fruitful practice might also have value for others. I began to shape my entries into devotional reflections; this books contains fifty-two of them. In the spirit of Al-Anon and its emphasis on protecting our loved ones' privacy, I am writing under a pseudonym.

I have felt greatly blessed to work on this project; so often I have sensed Jesus' presence in genuinely transformative ways. As I've gained perspective on many destructive emotions that trapped me, the Holy Spirit has inspired me to think more creatively about Carl's and my situation. One huge gift has come in my deeper love for my husband as I focus increasingly on his many fine qualities and on the ways our marriage enriches my life.

Carl too has been changing in ways that testify to God's intervention, but that is his story to tell. Suffice it to say that our life together today differs greatly from the period reflected in these meditations. I've deliberately chosen not to revise them since I wanted readers to have the original prayer experiences that have proved so helpful. Our mutual growth has filled my heart with gratitude—both to God and to my husband—as I reflect on this time.

I am also grateful to many others. I think of my friend Theresa who offered help and support as I worked through the feelings I describe in these pages and of the fine women and men I have come to know in Al-Anon. I want to thank a few close friends (they know who they are!) who looked at some of these meditations in their early stages, giving me feedback and granting me permission to mention their experiences. My heartfelt gratitude goes to Evelyn Bence, both for encouraging me in my work and for referring me to Upper Room Books. I am deeply grateful to the staff of Upper Room Books, particularly editorial director Jeannie Crawford-Lee, who welcomed me so thoughtfully, and managing editor Rita Collett, who saw me through the editorial process with such enthusiasm and skill.

My profound gratitude goes to my husband, Carl. I realize that many spouses of addicted loved ones have no choice but to leave for the sake of self-preservation or their children's welfare, and I specifically address their concerns in some of the reflections. In my own case, though, Carl's faith amidst our struggles enabled me to stay. His love and support, his willingness to forgive me time and again for the turbulence that often engulfed me as I faced our shared challenges helped us to grow together. When

I learned the manuscript had been accepted for publication, I felt understandably apprehensive about whether he would want me to proceed. Rather than asking me to stop, he gave his blessing to the project, and for this I thank him from the bottom of my heart.

INTRODUCTION

GERALD MAY, the late psychiatrist and spiritual counselor, says our deepest desire is an inborn longing for God's love. But things go wrong. Without realizing it, we can attach the energy of this longing to something other than God. Before long that "something" begins to take over, destroying our freedom and forcing our relationship with God into second place. May suggests in the first chapter of *Addiction and Grace* that left to our own devices we are all "addicted" in this sense, one way or another, even if our habits or thought patterns appear quite harmless.

Our personal addictions become more complicated when we also deal with the addictions of family members or friends, some of which may be seriously damaging, like alcoholism or drug abuse. We probably know what it's like to encounter our own demons that our loved ones' addictions call forth. We may have vowed never again to collapse in tears or fly into a rage or freeze in guilty paralysis, only to find ourselves repeatedly doing just that. Like our loved ones, we're helpless to change by relying on our strength alone. We need God's grace.

These meditations relate my journey as I sought that grace through scripture while struggling to cope with my husband's drinking. The passages that inspire them come from all four Gospels. They depict significant moments in

Jesus' life and ministry arranged here in rough chronological sequence as they appear in the Bible, beginning with his birth and ending with the Great Commission. Each reflection opens with a brief summary of the entire passage in biblical context before focusing on a few words—a phrase, a sentence, a whole verse—that seemed highlighted for me at the time and that drew me into prayer about circumstances I faced then.

I present the scripture passages chronologically rather than organizing them by topic because I encountered them in this fashion. *A Harmony of the Four Gospels* (using the New International Version of the Bible) by Orville E. Daniel formed the basis of my study. It arranges the content of Matthew, Mark, Luke, and John into four separate columns on each page so that similar passages stand side by side. Daniel then highlights selected phrases or sentences and sometimes entire paragraphs in darker bold-faced type to create a single narrative thread, a single story line that weaves back and forth among the different columns. This format allows a person to read from start to finish like a Gospel novella.

I hadn't anticipated the spiritual implications of this approach to Bible study. Rather than focusing on my specific need, I found myself centering on Jesus' unfolding life and ministry. As I delved deeper into scripture, that focus remained. I felt as if I was encountering the Lord personally in the context of a spiritual story larger than my own—much like the men and women about whom I was reading. The insights that broke over me in prayer seemed given by the Holy Spirit and touched me in ways I would probably not have sought on my own initiative.

Reading John 5:6, for example, where Jesus asks the invalid by the pool if he wants to get well, what first came to mind was how often I had wanted to ask my husband that same question (in a voice heavy with irony). Immediately I recognized the judgmentalism in my heart. Clearly the better question was whether I myself wanted to get well and stop brooding over my husband's drinking. The thought came straight out of Al-Anon with its stress on taking responsibility for ourselves rather than obsessing over the alcoholic. Now, though, living imaginatively into that Gospel scene, I experienced something beyond mere intellectual insight; I felt Another doing a powerful work in my heart—my frequent experience during this prayer adventure.

I hope this book's reflections will help readers in their own struggles with addicted loved ones, either as they read them alone or as they share them in a group. Even more than this, I hope the reflections will inspire others to reach out to Jesus themselves, just as I did. Each journey is unique, and no one's personal experience can provide the blueprint for another's pathway to growth. When we encounter the Lord through scripture, he will meet us where we are with the healing insights we need.

We can browse the text of any Bible translation till we find ourselves drawn to a particular phrase, sentence, or paragraph. Then we ask the Holy Spirit what message is hidden for us there, what nugget of healing awaits our discovery as we pray into those words and reflect on their implications.

For those of us dealing with a loved one's addiction, we may find the Lord showing us our own addictions to self-serving habits and assumptions that camouflage buried feelings and fuel dysfunctional responses. Getting in touch with these and drawing on God's grace to grow beyond them will support our own recovery as we learn to love in spiritually healthier ways. I pray that you too will experience Jesus' grace and guidance in your personal struggles with addicted loved ones as you read the meditations in these pages and as you reach out to him through your own scriptural reflections.

1

When Our Words Become Flesh

JOHN 1:1-3, 14

In the beginning was the Word. . . .

IN THE BEGINNING . . . God created the heavens and the earth," Genesis 1:1 tells us. Now, as the Fourth Gospel opens, the writer makes it plain that Christ himself—"the Word"—was there "in the beginning," in cocreative power with the Father. Then, in deliberate parallel to Genesis 1, John announces a radical new act of creation: The Word is made flesh, and Jesus comes to live among us. Yet even as he immerses himself in the struggles of humanity, Jesus mysteriously remains God incarnate. How he must grieve, knowing our potential for beauty, faith, and love even as he encounters the magnitude of the sin into which we fall!

Sin hurts. I know my own pain, both over my husband's drinking and over the gap between the way God wants me to respond to his behavior and the ways I actually do respond. From conversations with others, I also know something of the pain that they carry related to the destructive behavior that entraps their loved ones and their own inability to embody the "tough love" they long to convey. Parents agonize over addicted daughters and sons; adult children of alcoholics wrestle with dysfunction rooted in their earlier lives. If awareness of human failures can cause such pain, how much deeper must Jesus' pain have been over the sinfulness he encountered on earth!

Still, despite occasional outbursts of frustration recorded in the Gospels, Jesus never gives up on us. Along with perfect knowledge, he exhibits perfect love: He is full of grace and truth. He calls us on our sin without becoming enmeshed in difficult relationships. This capacity of Jesus stands in striking contrast to our own flawed ways of relating. God knows the ease with which we get enmeshed, especially as we struggle in relationships with loved ones. Our turbulent feelings of anger, despair, or shame can overwhelm us, sloshing over onto the other person and contaminating our attempts to speak healing insights into those loved ones' lives.

Jesus' intimacy with Abba allowed him to love in a pure way, keeping him centered, harmonizing his words and deeds. Never did he say one thing and act out another.

It's reassuring to be with people who are so close to the Lord that their words "become flesh" when we are with them. We perceive perfect harmony between their words and the way that they treat us. God sent me a dear friend many years ago when my whole world was collapsing around me as my first husband was breaking away from our marriage. At that vulnerable time, this friend assured me that Jesus loved me and would never leave me, and I was able to believe her. Her words rang true because in her presence I experienced the embodied reality of that love.

How many times have we tried—and failed—to speak "the truth in love" (Eph. 4:15)? But what if parents who must ask an addicted son or daughter to leave the house unless he or she get help could state this simply and clearly? What if one friend could calmly confront another about a disturbing habit? What if one spouse could voice his or her concern to the other without getting entangled in anxiety and resentment? What if I could do this with my own husband? May all of us grow in our capacity to speak the truth as Jesus does—one step at a time.

Prayer

God, we thank you for the gift of the Incarnation and Jesus' redemptive death that cleanses us of our sin. Thank you for forgiving both us and our loved ones when we repeatedly fail to live and love as you call us. Help us draw closer to you day by day so that our words of caring and concern can truly become flesh for the ones we love. Amen.

2

Turning toward the Light

JOHN 1:4-5, 9-13

*The light shines in the darkness, and the
darkness did not overcome it.*

THE IMAGERY OF LIGHT floods both John's Gospel
and his epistles. Indeed, the entire Bible shines with ref-
erences to light. Just as Isaiah 49:6 announces God's call
for God's servant people to be the light of the world, so
Jesus—God incarnate and the embodied servant promised
by Isaiah—comes into the world as that light. Moreover,
Jesus calls each of us to be light: "You are the light of the
world" (Matt. 5:14).

In our everyday lives we speak metaphorically about
many kinds of light that God offers to dispel our darkness:
the light of truth over falsehood, clarity over confusion,
hope over hopelessness, faith over despair, and love over
resentment. Sometimes, however, we don't desire God's
light. Sometimes we choose to remain in the darkness of
confusion and denial.

Why would we want that? Why wouldn't we prefer
to live in the light of truth, clarity, hope, faith, and love?
When we choose God's light, we can never predict which

of our cherished agendas or self-images God will ask us to give up. We realize, if only subconsciously, that the Lord will challenge many of our habits and assumptions. We can easily focus on our *loved ones'* need to renounce denial and choose the light of truth. But what about us?

I too am prone to denial, especially when it comes to looking honestly at Carl's struggles and the ways that I compound them with my behavior. Many of us resist accepting the full truth about our loved ones' addictions and our own dysfunctional responses. Perhaps we want to believe it's a simple matter of their making the right moral choice and exercising willpower, which we have every right to expect them to do—becoming angry when they don't. If we don't react with anger, maybe we tell ourselves that if we just try harder to please an addicted family member, everything will get better, or if we weep over how much the behavior is hurting us, our weeping will do the trick. Then again, we may feel convinced that we can control a loved one by monitoring every move. Whatever our characteristic response happens to be, when we react from a place of denial, we succumb to a darkness of our own.

The New Revised Standard Version and the latest edition of the New International Version (NIV) tell us in their translations of John 1:5 that the darkness has not "overcome" the light. Earlier editions of the NIV translate this verse to read, "The light shines in the darkness, but the darkness has not understood it." Both translations bear witness to truth. In the darkness of denial we may think we understand what is happening, but this only reflects our pseudo-understanding. Even when we turn our backs on an honest confrontation with reality, God's light continues to shine. Our preference for darkness and denial can never overcome the radiance of that light. I greatly appreciate the words of Psalm 139:

> If I say, "Surely the darkness shall cover me,
>   and the light around me become night,"
> even the darkness is not dark to you;
>   the night is as bright as the day,
>   for darkness is as light to you (vv. 11-12).

On this side of heaven we always see dimly, as in a mirror. But we can choose to turn toward God's light rather than remain in darkness, and we can ask the Holy Spirit to open the eyes of our hearts to receive that light ever more fully, day by day. Then we can begin to embrace the truth, clarity, hope, faith, and love that Jesus offers.

PRAYER
Thank you, Lord, for shining your light into the darkness of our lives. Thank you that our ignorance and resistance can never extinguish it, even though we sometimes choose to turn away from your radiance. As we live with our loved ones, give us the desire and courage to seek your light: the light of truth over falsehood, of clarity over confusion, of hope over hopelessness, of faith over despair, and of love over resentment. Amen.

3

Clinging to God's Promises

*"Blessed is she who believed that there would be a
fulfillment of what was spoken to her by the Lord."*

W<small>HEN THE ANGEL</small> G<small>ABRIEL</small> visits Mary and announces
that she, a virgin, will give birth to the "Son of the Most
High" by the power of the Holy Spirit, Mary accepts this
strange and frightening message: "Here am I, the servant
of the Lord; let it be with me according to your word."
Arriving at the home of Elizabeth, her pregnant relative,
Mary must feel overcome with awe when Elizabeth tells
her that the baby in her own womb leaped for joy at the
sound of Mary's greeting. Then Elizabeth speaks these
words: "Blessed is she who believed that there would be a
fulfillment of what was spoken to her by the Lord."

Mary believes a message that promises a supernatural
event, which seems foreign to our lives. What about us?
Have we "heard" deep in our hearts a promise or a word
from God—a word about our troubled loved ones?

We may find it hard to discern whether such messages
come from God or are simply the voices of our hopes and
dreams. Maybe a promise related to growth and recovery

didn't come true. Or we may have followed a course of action that we believed God called us to and been horrified by the consequences. One friend told me that she had married her husband in response to a God-given word, only to learn after their marriage that her husband had resumed his preengagement pattern of heavy drinking. For three years she cried out to the Lord, asking why God had told her to marry this man! Thankfully, her husband did find sobriety, but outcomes are not always this happy.

Either way, we need to acknowledge the Bible as our foundational resource when it comes to identifying God's promises. Scripture is rich with principles that describe God's work in human lives—core principles that have proven trustworthy time and again in the experience of believers who stake their lives on them, trusting them as bedrock guides. Consider Romans 8:28 ("We know that all things work together for good for those who love God, who are called according to his purpose") or the promise in Philippians 1:6 that "the one who began a good work among you will bring it to completion by the day of Jesus Christ." Promises like these don't identify or point us toward a specific outcome ahead of time. They don't give us a particular image of what to expect or when to expect it, lest its failure to "come true" right away dash our hopes. Rather, they build a basic attitude of trust. They nurture a personal stance of faith and endurance that will strengthen us over time and heighten our sensitivity to God's activity in our lives.

Paul tells us in Philippians 4:11 that he has learned to be content with whatever befalls him. Doesn't this sound like Al-Anon's assurance that contentment and happiness are possible even if the alcoholics in our lives continue to drink? I remember my skepticism when someone spoke those words at my first meeting. Now I know from experience that the habit of grounding myself in core biblical promises has helped me take baby steps toward this sort of contentment.

A best practice for those of us with addicted loved ones comes in immersing ourselves in scripture, seeking out and clinging to the specific promises that resonate in our hearts. As we discover the ones that speak to us and make them our own by repeating them to ourselves during the tough times, God will give us the faith and trust to stake our lives on them.

Prayer

We praise you, O God, for your promises in the Bible. Lead us by your Holy Spirit to the promises we need in our own struggles. Then help us take them into our hearts so they become our bedrock guides when discouragement and confusion cause us to doubt. We pray this in Jesus' name. Amen.

4

From Pride to Vulnerability

LUKE 1:46-55

*[God] has scattered the proud
in the thoughts of their hearts.*

THE WORDS OF THE MAGNIFICAT, Mary's song of praise in response to Elizabeth's unborn baby leaping for joy upon Mary's arrival, are some of the most glorious in scripture. A multitude of images adorn the Magnificat. But today this single sentence seems highlighted for me, and instinctively I find myself listening to it in my mind's ear in the majestic poetry of the King James version: "[God] hath scattered the proud in the imagination of their hearts." Now I recall a passage from Daniel 4. There Nebuchadnezzar of Babylon, in fulfillment of Daniel's prophecy, succumbs to pride in his own majesty and is toppled from the throne, driven into exile in the wilderness. For a season he lives with the wild beasts, disintegrated and mad, his hair growing like birds' feathers and his nails like claws. Not until he raises his eyes to heaven and recognizes the Lord as ruler over all does his reason return to him. As he acknowledges God's glory, his kingdom is restored.

This is a much grander and more dramatic example of the scattering of the proud than most of us will encounter! Yet, in smaller ways Mary's words may hit home in our own lives. Everyone is subject to the sin of pride. Speaking for myself, emotionally a part of me wants to feel invulnerable, never mind how this flies in the face of reality. I want to escape all life's slings and arrows. On some primitive level I react as though I deserve special consideration!

During the first months of marriage, as I began to realize how my husband's drinking would impact our shared life, I tried to kid myself that I could retain control over our circumstances. When I began to attend Al-Anon meetings and heard that those of us living with addicted loved ones were meant to accept that we were powerless over alcohol and our lives had become unmanageable, I fought that idea with every ounce of my energy: *I'm not powerless! My husband, maybe—but not I! I am in control of my life!* Surely these thoughts spring from pride.

Few of us with addicted loved ones suffer the same kind or degree of addiction that enslaves them. Still, in May's sense of the term, we are all addicts of one sort or another. Aren't we bound by assumptions about ourselves and our rights that we don't question? Such assumptions can fuel all manner of emotional reactions—anger, panic, or despair—that too easily take us over.

It's easy to point to our loved ones' pride in the pretense that they're in charge of their behavior when clearly they're not. But we also display a similar pride when we cherish the idea that we deserve to live a problem-free life or persist in the belief we can control another's addiction.

Yes, ego strength is a good thing, and, yes, it's healthy to develop and practice skills associated with responsible adult living. But we never ultimately control anything in our lives. Sickness or disaster can strike at any moment. The power we feel we have is superficial at best.

By clinging to an illusion of control, we reject the gifts of the Holy Spirit. Genuine faith implies ultimate dependence on God each and every moment, regardless of the situation or circumstance. Only by doing so can we also love our neighbors as ourselves, for to covet autonomy is to set ourselves apart from the human condition. So when prideful desire to be in charge begins to surface, events that scatter and shake us into new configurations can sometimes be blessings from God.

PRAYER

O God, we confess our own pride and the ways we allow it to lead us into self-centered styles of thought and action that do not honor you. Especially we confess our willingness to cling to illusions of control in relationships with our loved ones. Help us rid our lives of the idol of autonomy. We repent and turn to you with newly humbled hearts. In Jesus' name. Amen.

5

The Treasure of Memories

LUKE 2:8-20

*Mary treasured all these words and pondered
them in her heart.*

MARY'S IMMEDIATE TREASURE here is the testimony
of the shepherds who have hurried to Bethlehem to find
and worship the newborn baby whom the angel identified
as their "Savior, . . . the Messiah, the Lord." Just trying
to encompass everything Mary has been given to ponder
regarding Jesus' birth—the Annunciation, the awe-filled
meeting with her relative Elizabeth, and now this strange
reverential visit from the shepherds—stretches our imagination to the breaking point.

"Mary treasured all these words and pondered them in
her heart." Thinking ahead to Jesus' adult years and all that
his mother would witness of his unfolding ministry and
eventual crucifixion, we can imagine how many times she
recalled those events surrounding his birth, turning them
over and over in memory, gathering courage and inspira-
tion to meet the challenges to her faith and the stretching
and shattering of her heart.

What personal memories do we treasure and revisit when we find our faith challenged? I remember one afternoon in the local bookstore a month or so before marrying as I struggled with doubts about proceeding. Nestled in a big overstuffed armchair I was reading Ephesians 5:21-33, which offers a vision of Christian marriage. The verses about wifely submission and husbandly "headship" had often raised my hackles in the past. Suddenly, as I gazed out the huge window at the setting sun and the hazy lights in the parking lot, the words commanding the husband to love his wife as Christ loves the church struck me as if for the first time. What would it be like to be loved in this way, to experience the sacrificial love of Jesus embodied in my marriage? Of course I would want to "submit"—to abandon myself in trust—in such a union! I felt transported into a mystical space of beauty beyond description. I didn't understand it rationally, and I still don't. But in that moment all my hesitation about proceeding with the wedding dissolved. Driving home later, though, doubts began to assail me. As I asked the Lord if I could trust that bookstore experience, a sense of peace flooded over me.

Often since that day I have wondered: *What was that afternoon all about? Was God giving me a message that over the years, despite the challenges we would face, ultimately my husband and I would grow into this kind of union? Or was I being given an image to help me understand metaphorically the way that Jesus loves us and the kind of submitted trust to which we are called in return?* I find myself thinking today that it was probably the latter. Still, who knows what the future holds? I do know that whenever I reflect on experience of that afternoon, I always find comfort.

Many of us have memories like this: a time when we saw a wave of vulnerability break over a child's face or heard a word of affirmation from a hitherto silent parent. Even seemingly bad memories—of a loved one explaining a need to pull away from us, for instance—can bear the seeds of healing insights as we revisit them. So in times of dismay and bewilderment over our circumstances, we can return to the memories we treasure in our hearts, finding in them a comfort that renews our faith.

PRAYER

Dear God, we thank you for precious memories that comfort us in times of sorrow and challenge us in times of doubt. We don't understand your activity and presence in those times, but we recognize the blessings these memories have bestowed on us in our struggles. Guide us as we revisit them over the years, always finding the encouragement to trust you and to place our future in your hands. Amen.

6

The Challenge of Obedience

LUKE 2:41-51

*Then [Jesus] went down with them and came to Nazareth,
and was obedient to them.*

As THEY DO EACH YEAR, Jesus' parents take him to
Jerusalem for the Feast of the Passover. This time, however, presumably returning with a large party of extended
family, they don't realize till they have started home that
Jesus isn't with them. Frantic, they retrace their steps and
discover him in the Temple talking with the teachers. Mary
asks why he has terrified them so, only to receive the cryp-
tic reply: "Did you not know that I must be in my Father's
house?" Then he returns home with them and is "obedient
to them."

Why does this word *obedient* fly out at me? The Gospel narrative addresses Jesus' obedience as a child, but my
mind leaps to other matters. Certainly if the addicts we
love are Christian, we may agonize over what we see as
their lack of obedience when it comes to dealing with
temptation. However, recovery guidelines would counsel
us to focus on ourselves instead. So now I ponder the question of *my* personal obedience or my lack of it. And here's

the rub. I uncover a lot of resistance inside myself to the notion of obedience as we sometimes understand it.

How exactly are we meant to obey? So often we may feel pressure to take a scriptural command out of context and try to obey it in legalistic fashion. But what does Jesus say about obedience? "If you love me, you will keep my commandments," he tells us in John 14:15. Interestingly, as I read these words, the idea of obedience no longer troubles me. This verse focuses on our relationship with Jesus and the importance of moving into deeper intimacy with him. Obedience in this sense differs from impersonally following a set of rules. Indeed, in the biblical setting of this verse—Jesus' farewell discourse to his disciples before his crucifixion—the underlying theme is our call to love one another. The more I pray into such passages, the more they remind me of others in the Gospels where Jesus invites people to follow him. And Jesus' invitations to follow inspire me even as they present huge challenges. Once again, the focus is clearly relational.

One area in which I feel the Lord's strong call to follow and obey comes in taking a long objective look at my husband. I can sense in my spirit that Jesus calls me to accept the reality of everything about him and his struggles. Surely this reflects Jesus' desire for all who face challenges with those we love.

Jesus does not call us to agree that everything is OK but to face the whole truth with absolute honesty, putting away resentment, denial, judgmentalism, or fear and prayerfully seeking a greater understanding of our loved ones' temptations. We bring our shame, anger, grief, and anxiety to Jesus. We surrender all dreams of curing or fixing the loved ones in our lives and all attempts to manipulate or control.

I know that often I simply focus on how my husband's drinking impacts me rather than on its spiritual and physical implications for him. Moreover, when I give way to undisciplined emotionality, I exhibit my own disobedience. My concern about his being more obedient should prompt my recommitment to following Jesus faithfully and keeping my husband in prayer.

Deep down, I know that this obedience will bring me not only into richer intimacy with the Lord but also into a more mature agape love for my husband.

Prayer

O Lord, we resist full surrender and obedience to you, even though we acknowledge in our spirits that only in relationship with you can we discover true freedom. Give us the grace to long for such intimacy with you that we respond with joy when you call us to follow and obey you as Savior and Lord in our relationships with struggling loved ones. Amen.

7

The "Wild Beasts" of Temptation

MARK 1:9-13

The Spirit immediately drove [Jesus] out into
the wilderness . . . and he was with the wild beasts.

JESUS HAS JUST HAD a taste of what the late psychologist Abraham Maslow called a "peak experience." Emerging from the waters of baptism, he has seen the heavens open and the Spirit descend on him like a dove. He has heard God's voice proclaim, "You are my Son, the Beloved; with you I am well pleased." It's striking that *immediately* after this experience, the Holy Spirit drives Jesus out into the desert to face Satan's temptations. There, significantly, he finds himself "with the wild beasts." This added detail of "wild beasts" gives a particular chill to the story.

What do wild beasts mean to us? I recall my teen years of rebellion against my devoted mother. One morning she emerged from her bedroom. "I had the most awful nightmare," she told me. "I was walking a pack of dogs when they suddenly turned wild and began snapping at me, fighting their leashes and pulling me out of control." Her dream hit me hard, for I interpreted it as symbolic of our fight the night before.

When the Holy Spirit drives Jesus into the desert to face temptation after his baptism, we might expect that the temptations would appeal to the primitive aspects of his human nature. Out in the desert apart from civilized society, famished and with nothing standing between him and the "wild beasts" within and without, he is at his most vulnerable. We know that Jesus met that test with integrity, never giving way to the taunts Satan flung at him. But we don't always fare so well when challenges like that overwhelm us. Those of us with volatile temperaments can have a difficult time when the "wild beasts" that snap and snarl at us in our loved ones' emotions and in our own shatter our equilibrium.

When these emotional wild beasts confront us, we can turn to Jesus and focus on him intentionally. I know what it feels like to be caught up in the anger and desperation of the moment. Everything else vanishes from consciousness, and the words flying out of my mouth have a life of their own. If we quickly urge our loved ones to focus on Jesus when temptation strikes, we may not be nearly as ready ourselves to "take every thought captive to obey Christ" (2 Cor. 10:5) when wild beasts of anger and frustration come unbidden from our hearts.

Yet we can learn to turn immediately to Jesus. We can remember the self-discipline available to us in the Lord. We can be confident that the One who met his own temptations in the wilderness and took control over natural energies time and again in his earthly ministry—calming a storm at sea or walking on the waves—is always with us, ready to strengthen us and help us curb unruly responses.

One final thought. For some people, the wild behavior that's front and center in life with an addict or otherwise disturbed individual takes the form of actual physical violence. The first response to such threats: Move from harm's way to seek protection. There will be time enough later for dealing with the spiritual and emotional wreckage such abuse causes. It's crucial to remember that no one deserves such treatment; physical abuse is never God's will.

Prayer

Lord Jesus, you remained strong when you faced temptation, but often we fall prey to the wild beasts of our destructive emotions or volatile behavior in life with addicted loved ones. When we face any danger, help us to turn to you in obedience and find protection, steadiness, and balance. Amen.

8

Discerning God's Authentic Call

MATTHEW 4:1-11

"If you are the Son of God. . . ."

TEMPTING JESUS IN THE DESERT wilderness, Satan repeatedly begins with these words: "If you are the Son of God. . . ." He needn't have used the conditional *if.* He could have said, "*Since* you are the Son of God. . . ." and conveyed an entirely different meaning. That little word *if* is critical. Yes, Satan wants Jesus to misuse his power by turning stones into bread, by provoking God's supernatural intervention as he hurls himself off the pinnacle of the Temple, or by choosing secular riches and fame and renouncing his allegiance to the Father. Satan's primary objective, though, is probably to make Jesus doubt the validity of his baptismal experience. He wants Jesus to question his core identity as the Son of God. And Jesus is genuinely vulnerable here—alone, exhausted, and famished. Yet he comes to the wilderness fresh from his peak experience of seeing the Spirit descend on him like a dove and hearing God's voice proclaim, "You are my Son, the Beloved; with you I am well pleased."

Some of us know firsthand how our euphoria of believing we've received a call from God can leave us vulnerable in its aftermath. I know I do. One afternoon while browsing through the *Life Recovery Bible*, I glanced at a sidebar designed to bring readers to a biblical understanding of Step 10 in the 12-Step program, "We continued to take personal inventory and when we were wrong promptly admitted it." It drew attention to Romans 5:3-5, where Paul reminds us that our trials produce endurance, strength of character, and hope. In an encouraging spin on these verses, the editors urged readers not to lose heart, even after repeated falls, but to approach each relapse as a new opportunity to rely on God's forgiveness and receive strength for the future.

I had been berating myself for having lost my temper (again!) the previous night. But while reading the words of the sidebar, an awesome sense of grace washed over me. What if the Lord was calling me to embody this principle for my husband by meeting him in a loving spirit of calm and peace and giving him an opportunity to experience divine forgiveness and encouragement . . . through me! It felt like a bolt out of the blue—a true spiritual high.

You can guess what happened. Quite in contrast to Jesus' strength under Satan's attack, the next time I found my husband drinking, that memory dissolved in a flash, and I heard angry words coming out of my mouth.

So what lesson did the Lord teach me? Looking back, I realize my vulnerability had a double edge. On the one hand, I experienced the natural letdown that comes after a "high"; but on the other hand, I had certainly misunderstood God's message. Al-Anon stresses the "three Cs" when it comes to a loved one's addiction—we didn't *cause* it, we can't *control* it, we can't *cure* it. Yes, I experienced a trustworthy sense of grace that day, but my interpretation of the experience surely was not. The Lord couldn't have been calling me to codependency by asking me to heal my husband magically and heroically or by perfecting my own behavior. More likely Jesus was encouraging me to appropriate that guideline from Romans for myself and to see my relapses into turbulence as fresh chances to receive and be strengthened by God's forgiveness in my life.

Now that is a deeply comforting thought that truly feels right.

PRAYER
At your baptism, Lord, you saw the Spirit descend like a dove, declaring you to be the beloved Son of the Most High. When our peak experiences come, give us clarity and wisdom to discern your word. Then strengthen us for obedience. Amen.

The Life Recovery Bible, New Living Translation, 2nd ed. (Carol Stream, IL: Tyndale House Publishers, 2007), 1441.

9

Feeding on God's Word

MATTHEW 4:1-11

"One does not live by bread alone, but by every word that comes from the mouth of God."

T HIS SCRIPTURAL AFFIRMATION is Jesus' response to the first temptation Satan flings at him after Jesus' baptism and forty days in the wilderness. "Command these stones to become loaves of bread," Satan has just demanded.

At the Church of the Saviour, a radically faithful ecumenical community in Washington, DC, the late pastor Gordon Cosby preached over the years about our temptation to turn stones into bread by grounding ourselves in all manner of "false securities" (job, money, status) as substitutes for the soul-deep identity only a relationship with God can provide. Cosby even suggested we can become "cultural addicts" when we give way repeatedly to this temptation! Just as an alcoholic may need daily AA meetings to stay sober, so we (especially those of us struggling to cope with a loved one's addiction) will need consistent biblically grounded fellowship with other believers to stay anchored in discipleship to Jesus.

Studying scripture by yourself can also be life-changing. When my first marriage was breaking up against my will and I was coming to faith in Jesus, I used to immerse myself in the Bible night after night. Particular verses would leap out at me during those long evenings, as though begging for my attention. Sometimes it came as a hard biblical challenge like "Do not judge, so that you may not be judged" (Matt. 7:1); at other times I received an encouraging promise, like "Blessed are those who mourn, for they will be comforted" (Matt. 5:4). Both the challenges and the promises, the disturbing words and the comforting ones, carried significance. Together they stirred a creative tension in my heart that birthed me into new growth. Before long I found I desperately needed other Christians with whom to explore scripture. Propelled by this need, I found my way to a church whose members reached out to me with love and compassion, drawing me into several Bible studies that nourished me at that precarious time in my life.

At that point in my faith journey I was struggling with the major crisis of a disintegrating marriage. Now, living into the different challenges my life poses, I have been experiencing the same profound relationship with scripture as I pray through these gospel reflections.

A dear friend recently shared with me how she sought help to work on her marriage because she believed God wanted her to remain with her husband despite his drinking. In her case Al-Anon didn't seem to be meeting her needs, but she did discover a Bible-based prayer and support group for women struggling in spiritually mismatched marriages. Her membership in this group turned out to be critical. Years later her husband did come to sobriety and, with much hard work over time, their union grew steadily stronger. To this day she remains convinced that the prayerful study of scripture with those caring women carried her through. Together, they helped one another feed on "every word that comes from the mouth of God."

Prayer

Lord Jesus, when Satan tempted you in the wilderness following your baptism, you turned repeatedly to scripture for the strength to resist. Help us also to turn to scripture for wisdom, encouragement, and clarity in struggles with our loved ones. May we live "by every word that comes from the mouth of God," and give us trustworthy and wise sisters and brothers in Christ to nurture and support us along this journey. Amen.

10

When We Can't Seem to Grow

JOHN 3:1-16

"How can anyone be born after having grown old?"

Nicodemus, a Pharisee of Jerusalem, comes to Jesus at night. He doesn't open their conversation with a question. He simply acknowledges that he understands who Jesus is—"for no one can do these signs that you do apart from the presence of God." Jesus' enigmatic reply honors Nicodemus's witness. "Very truly, I tell you, no one can see the kingdom of God without being born from above."

Together with John 3:16, "'God so loved the world that he gave his only Son, so that everyone who believes in him may not perish but may have eternal life,'" evangelical Christians believe that what is at stake here is our eternal destiny. John 17:3—"This is eternal life, that they may know you, the only true God, and Jesus Christ whom you have sent"—implies that scripture also asks us to view eternal life as a radically new dimension of living we can begin to experience right here and now.

Nicodemus thinks in literal terms when he asks his question, but we know that Jesus isn't speaking literally. Describing spiritual rebirth, he uses the language of poetry:

"The wind blows where it chooses, and you hear the sound of it, but you do not know where it comes from or where it goes. So it is with everyone who is born of the Spirit." Jesus invites Nicodemus to trust him in a whole new way so he can begin to know the kind of glorious transformed living that is indeed eternal life.

And this raises troubling questions. Why do some of us, despite our relationship with Jesus, stay emotionally stuck over the years? Why are we unable to break through spiritual and emotional barriers that keep us from experiencing the radical new life Jesus describes?

What's holding us back? Do our old patterns feel so much a part of us that we can't imagine life without them? Would we rather stay with the familiar than dare to step out into new adventures of "kingdom living"? Going to heaven when we die isn't the issue here. The issue is whether we want to experience intimacy with Jesus right now and sense his immediate presence in our lives. What would it feel like to long so desperately for this intimacy and for the new beginning Jesus promises that any despair over the possibility of change might, by God's grace, be transformed into a new capacity for surrender?

Perhaps we're so discouraged by past failures that we honestly don't believe transformation can occur. We may fear disappointing ourselves, the Lord, and everyone else all over again. We may even question whether God can truly love us!

If we're caught in this trap, we can find liberation with God's help. First, we can ask Jesus to give us a taste of true intimacy with him to whet our appetite for more. Then we can reflect on the depth of his love for us and his limitless capacity to forgive, asking the Holy Spirit to direct us to passages in scripture that will bring this truth to life for us in our hearts as well as in our minds.

PRAYER

Thank you, Lord Jesus, that after our new birth you invite us and our loved ones to enter your kingdom realm here and now, to develop a closer relationship with you. In our sin and frailty, we often resist. Help us to long so deeply for intimacy with you that we surrender despite ourselves, breaking through ingrained patterns of fear and pride that have enslaved us over the years. May we come to understand the depth of your love and your eagerness to forgive our sins and draw us closer to you. Amen.

11

Radical Acceptance and Radical Challenge

JOHN 4:5-26

"Those who drink of the water that I will give them will never be thirsty."

JESUS' DIALOGUE WITH the Samaritan woman at the well becomes an ever-deepening encounter as the conversation unfolds. It opens simply enough, with Jesus asking for a drink and the woman expressing shock that he would violate custom by asking her—a Samaritan and a woman—to help him. Almost immediately, matters get more complicated as Jesus invites her to recognize him as Messiah and hints at the living water he can provide. She wants this gift badly enough that she not only asks for the living water but blurts out, "I have no husband" when he—who of course knows all about her anyway—asks her to get her husband and bring him there.

Acceptance is the key factor here. Jesus accepts her in a way she has never known before. But he also challenges her to grow in faith. The creative tension generated by his radical acceptance coupled with his radical challenge transforms her. Released from her previous sense of shame, she runs to tell people that she has met the Messiah.

When we come to Jesus in our vulnerability, we too can receive living water. Like the Samaritan woman, we may find ourselves broken open in new ways, facing truths about ourselves we've been reluctant to acknowledge. Many of us probably react with a characteristic emotional response—anger? depression? anxiety?—to the challenges of addicted loved ones' behavior. Whatever our customary reaction, we can safely assume that other feelings we may be unaware of lie beneath the surface.

Dealing with feelings can be tricky business. A psychology professor once stated that only four basic emotions exist: mad, sad, glad, and scared. One friend married to an alcoholic told me she never feels mad, only depressed; in other words, sad. I believe that some anger must lurk inside her and that getting in touch with it would increase her strength. Whenever I can bring my anger honestly to Jesus rather than defensively shutting myself away, he offers me the gift of greater self-awareness. In Jesus' presence I realize I'm feeling far more than anger. My heart aches with sadness at the contrast between Carl's condition when he's drunk and when he's sober. And the threats that addiction poses scare me. What if the damage to his body, mind, and spirit intensifies? What if his addictive behavior continues indefinitely, and I'm unable to handle it?

A physically abusive loved one, of course, allows no chance to camouflage fear. In *Waiting for His Heart: Les-*

sons from a Wife Who Chose to Stay, Joy McClain tells how she and her children often had to flee when safety became an issue; finally she obtained a legal separation and lived apart from her alcoholic husband until his eventual recovery and the restoration of their marriage. In situations like hers, the immediate need is clearly to secure protection. Only after reaching a place of safety can victims of physical abuse deal with its emotional repercussions.

Finally, what about the emotion of *joy*? It's probably no surprise this word doesn't pop up first thing when we look at responses to a loved one's disturbing behavior! Recently I've had occasional times not only of peace but also of joy, in a way that does indeed pass all understanding—joy in my relationship with Jesus but also in a renewed love and appreciation for my husband's fine qualities that I often ignore. This joy doesn't prevent anger, sadness, or fear from resurfacing, but it replenishes my heart with living water that buoys me up to face ongoing challenges.

Prayer

Thank you, Lord Jesus, that in your presence we experience your loving acceptance and your loving challenge to grow. May we be open and transparent with you, bringing to your presence feelings we have buried so that you can mold us into new creations. Give us your living water, and teach us to care for ourselves and our loved ones in more fruitful ways. Amen.

12

Embracing Repentance

MARK 1:14-15

*"The kingdom of God has come near; repent,
and believe in the good news."*

IN JOHN'S GOSPEL, Jesus generally announces his
identity as Messiah and challenges people to believe in him
rather than first asking them to repent. Here in Mark, the
call to repent introduces the call to believe. It interests me
that in the 12-Steps, foundational repentance—realizing
we are powerless over alcohol and other addictions (Step
1)—precedes full recognition of and surrender to God.
After this, subsequent steps call us to repent more specifically over time for particular ongoing failings.

How is accepting our powerlessness a foundational
form of repentance? We exhibit sinful pride when we cling
to the illusion that we can control the course of anyone's
addictions—including our own! Idolatry: the subcon-
scious belief that we can be on top of both our loved ones'
behavior and our own messy responses. A variation on this
theme includes kidding ourselves that every crisis will be
the key "bottoming-out" experience; or each time a loved
one breaks through to new insight, we may grab on to

premature hope. These responses often set us up for a fall of our own—back into anger or despair.

Tonight I need to repent. Recently my husband and I had a wonderful talk. I wanted so much to believe this talk signaled a permanent turnaround. When I came home a few days later to discover him drinking, I totally lost it. For that brief time I had been telling myself that our talk (which I had proudly helped to facilitate!) would surely enable him to choose sobriety.

"Repent, and believe in the good news," Jesus says. We need to keep reminding ourselves that the "good news" is not that our loved ones will find recovery or that an apparent breakthrough will promise permanent change. The good news Jesus offers us is our own opportunity for deeper kingdom living here and now, regardless of our loved ones' behaviors and activities. Part of our response comes not only in guarding against naive expectations of a cure each time we sense apparent breakthrough but also guarding against the opposite mistake of always waiting for the next shoe to drop, always anticipating the next plunge into drunkenness or drug abuse or whatever lies in wait just around the corner. Naïve optimism and obsessive mistrust are equally dangerous.

Jesus invites us into new realms of creative living if we will repent and believe. First, we repent of idolatrous illusions of control or unrealistic fantasies of instant cure; then we believe God will give us new gifts through the Holy Spirit if we renounce obsessive mistrust and risk open-ended faith. Rather than demanding a particular outcome, we take it on faith that God is working out a sovereign purpose in our lives amidst discouraging circumstances. God will continue to do so as we repeatedly place our trust in the divine will one day at a time.

Prayer

Dear Lord, help us to repent and believe the good news of your gospel ever more fully as time goes on. Deepen our understanding of the kingdom living you offer us. May our passion for this possibility keep our eyes focused on you and our trust in you steady and strong. Amen.

13

When Despair Overwhelms Us

John 4:46-53

"Sir, come down before my little boy dies."

THESE WORDS CONVEY both urgency and power—urgency on the part of the royal official whose son is dying and power on the part of Jesus. Hearing that Jesus has arrived in Cana where he recently performed his first miraculous sign by turning water into wine, this official hurries to him and begs him to heal his son. He is not dissuaded by Jesus' response, "Unless you see signs and wonders you will not believe." He continues to focus clearly on his need and repeats his request: "Sir, come down before my little boy dies." We sense that the man's single-minded focus and faith moves Jesus, for without further ado he grants the request: "Go; your son will live." The man takes Jesus at his word and departs.

I find myself powerfully moved by the stark simplicity of this man's need and his expression of it. In Al-Anon meetings, parents of addicted sons or daughters often express a similar urgency. Do they exercise "tough love" and make their beloved children leave the house if they refuse treatment? Or do they give them one more chance?

What should they do? What can they do? Then comes the most terrible possibility of all: What if they bear partial responsibility for the situation? How I've longed for those aching parents to feel loving arms around them in their despair! How I've wished Jesus could be present in the room to meet them with supernatural healing power!

And, of course, Jesus can be palpably present with us in extraordinary ways, often when we least expect it. I had such an experience myself one evening as I read this same Gospel passage.

After a long and difficult day, I felt drained, discouraged, depleted. It seemed that the whole issue of alcohol had demolished me, leaving me desperate for any help I could find. I read through this particular passage, trying to settle on a phrase or sentence over which to pray, but the words on the page seemed lifeless. In my desperation, I asked God to help me find some word or phrase in the reading that would speak to my condition. Then I read the passage again. As I did so, a single sentence leapt out at me. It was the man's simple and eloquent request as he turns to Jesus, "Sir, come down before my little boy dies."

This seemed a strange connection to me. So I asked, *Lord, what's going on here?* Then, after a moment, I raised an unexpected question in the silence of my heart: *Is there something in me that I fear is going to die?*

No sooner had I asked that question than I heard a quiet but clear answer: "You fear that your capacity to love is dying inside you." I knew the truth of those words.

At once I began to cry, and as the cleansing tears coursed down my cheeks, I could feel the Holy Spirit's presence with me in a powerful way. As I sat there quietly in the living room, I understood that a miracle had taken place. Instead of my previous depletion, there rose up in my heart a blessed feeling of peace—even a quiet joy. All memories of the day's struggles washed away, and in their place I felt gratitude for my husband's good qualities: his fidelity, his honesty, his enduring and solid faith in God despite his addiction, his willingness to forgive me time and again for my outbursts of anger. Gratitude flooded my heart, and I felt a deep and restored love for this man I married.

Prayer

Thank you, God, that your word is "living and active, sharper than any two-edged sword" (Heb. 4:12) and that it can pierce us and heal our hearts. Your love for us has not only enabled us to love but has also given us the assurance that we can turn to you when our capacity to love fails. Thank you for your presence with us in our need. You replenish our depleted hearts with your living water, restoring our love and giving us hope for the troubled ones in our lives. Amen.

14

Repenting, Believing, and Following

MATTHEW 4:18-22

"Follow me, and I will make you fish for people."

THIS PASSAGE DETAILS JESUS' CALL to Simon Peter and Andrew to follow him as disciples and closely parallels the account in Mark 1:16-20. We find a more fleshed-out version in Luke 5:1-11, where Jesus uses Simon's boat as a platform to teach, following which Simon brings in a miraculous catch of fish. In the versions of Matthew and Mark, we have no miraculous catch—only Jesus' call for the brothers to follow and an immediate response on their part. He issues an identical call to James and John a couple of verses farther on.

We come to Jesus in so many ways—believing, following, repenting, or through simple conversation like the one with the woman at the well. (See John 4:5-26.) However it happens, a relationship unfolds for each of us, uniquely designed to fit our personalities and needs. If we begin with belief, we will need to learn to repent and follow as we understand more. If we begin by following, then belief and repentance will need to deepen as our journey continues. Or repentance may precede both following and believing. Whatever the order, all three elements will eventually come into play in a full relationship with Jesus.

It's the same in our relationships with troubled loved ones. We come to believe that Jesus will heal us as we struggle with our own responses in these relationships. We repent of our failures when we fall victim to judgmentalism, despair, or a compulsion to compare our circumstances to others—each of which will overwhelm us and trip us up. And as best we can, we follow the path to which Jesus has called us as we navigate life together with our loved ones. Always we need to center ourselves in Jesus for guidance and strength.

As we discover in the Gospel narratives, these elements come in no formulaic order. Sometimes, two of them may blend into one. Repentance, for instance, may express itself through a new and sustained commitment to follow. Relationship with Jesus is holistic and organic. Jesus responded to everyone he encountered in a way that met each individual where he or she was at the time. The same holds true for us today.

I think of one friend who battled courageously to remain married, both during her husband's active alcoholism and for several years after he found sobriety. She always believed in Jesus' power to restore lives, but there had been so much pain in the marriage relationship that she found herself weeping at the slightest instigation (finding dirty socks on the floor) for a long, long time. She doesn't recall feeling judgmental toward her husband—nothing there requiring repentance—just pain, anxiety, distrust. Yet, she persisted in following the Lord, giving herself totally to rebuilding their marriage, even though she wanted out. Her commitment to Jesus bore fruit as the relationship strengthened and deepened over the years. I find her lack of judgmental anger remarkable, for I have had to repent time and again over this particular sin. I always recommit to follow, and my belief in Jesus continues to sustain me.

Each of us follows a unique path. The one consistent truth is that Jesus travels with us, meeting us where we are and guiding us into new growth.

PRAYER

Dear God, thank you for the Gospels that provide such a rich and colorful tapestry of the life and ministry of Jesus As we read these words of scripture, help us to find what we need to deepen our relationship with you. You know each of us and the places where we need to grow, especially in the challenges presented by our loved ones' struggles. Lead us to believe rightly, to repent fervently, and to follow fruitfully. Amen.

15

From Depletion to Restoration

Mark 1:32-34

The whole city was gathered around the door.

From the beginning of his public ministry, Jesus' authority amazes people, both in his teaching and his power to heal. "At once his fame began to spread throughout the surrounding region of Galilee," Mark tells us. One evening "the whole city" gathers at the door. We can only imagine Jesus' exhaustion as he faces such vast needs. For that reason, he so often takes time to be alone for restorative prayer.

When we struggle in relationships with our loved ones, we may often feel that we too live in the presence of exhausting needs. For Jesus, the huge crowds pressing in around him must have felt overwhelming. Ironically, for us, exhaustion may come from a sense of isolation and depletion as we seek to maintain our own stability amid personal chaos.

Just as Jesus needed to take time for solitary communion with his Abba, we also need to pull away for prayer and spiritual replenishment. It helps me to go somewhere alone and write in my journal or to confide in a close

Christian friend whose discretion I can trust. Others may find healing sitting in a garden or taking a long walk.

But other options exist. This may seem paradoxical, but it helps to shift attention away from our troubles to the needs of others—perhaps the very needs that overwhelm Jesus in this passage. Many churches have e-mail prayer groups through which folks can reach out both for prayer and for practical or relational aid. Or there may be opportunities to join in shared volunteer efforts like feeding the homeless or visiting shut-ins. When we collaborate with others to serve in this way, we often forge small communities where we can minister to one another in restorative ways, finding refreshment after exhaustion and gaining perspective on the struggles depleting us closer to home.

If we harbor a sense of shame over a loved one's addiction, we may hesitate to let ourselves be vulnerable enough to receive help from whose with whom we serve. *What would people think if they knew the whole truth?* I'm not suggesting that we share details that would compromise privacy. We can open our hearts and reach out for support without violating our loved ones' trust. "Well, it's been a tough week," we can say. "The details aren't important, though." Then we can listen—really listen—to our friends' words and take what we hear back to God in prayer.

The second great commandment in Matthew 22:39, where Jesus calls us to love our neighbors "as ourselves," has rich spiritual implications for those of us whose intimate relationships have left us depleted and exhausted. When we join others in mutual ministry, loving our neighbors as ourselves together, we often discover a new respect for our own self-worth; we discover a longing to grow into the people God wants us to be and a willingness to deal with the obstacles that hold us back. In such loving groups we experience the truth of how much God already loves and accepts us, and we realize that we can love only because he first loved us. (See 1 John 4:19.) With this realization we often receive the blessing of new hope that allows us to return to our private struggles with a renewed and refreshed spirit.

Prayer

Lord Jesus, in so many Gospel stories the crowds press in on you, clamoring for your healing touch. Often you went apart to seek fellowship with Abba and to find needed restoration. Help us, Lord, to learn from your example. Help us pull away for time alone when the chaos of life with our loved ones depletes us, and direct us toward renewal through fellowship and service with our Christian brothers and sisters. Amen.

16

How Do We Need to Be Healed?

JOHN 5:1-9

"Do you want to be made well?"

THE INVALID TO WHOM Jesus asks the above question has been lying thirty-eight years at the pool "called in Hebrew Beth-zatha," near the Sheep Gate. He cannot get to the healing waters since there is no one to help him. But Jesus offers a challenge. "Stand up, take your mat and walk," he says. At once the man does so—cured!

A phrase has been going through my head a lot these days: *the disease that is alcoholism.* Recovery literature tells us that it makes no more sense to judge the alcoholic's compulsion to drink than to judge a victim of cancer. Some people question the appropriateness of a "disease model" for alcoholism; but regardless of theoretical approach, most would agree that it's fruitless to judge another. Yet when I am honest, I have to admit that often I do judge. Not the compulsion to drink, not the temptation: No, of course I don't judge that. But I sometimes judge the ways my husband does—or doesn't—deal with that temptation. And I recall all the unsolicited and therefore useless advice I've tried to offer! "Why don't you carry some Bible verses around with you and whip them out when the urge to drink comes to mind?" Or more directly, with an ironic edge to my voice, "Don't you want to get well?" Deep down, I know that I actually need to ask myself two questions. First, what "disease" do I suffer from, metaphorically speaking? And second, do I really want to be made well?

In some ways my life was easier when my symptoms manifested in a physical way. During the first year of marriage, as I absorbed the implications of my husband's drinking problem, I couldn't feel my feelings. Instead I felt dizzy—very dizzy. And believe me, I wanted to get well! I found that taking brisk walks, repeating certain scripture verses to myself helped. I learned that identifying and naming my feelings—"I'm feeling mad right now; I'm feeling scared!"—helped as well. Now that those physical symptoms have lifted, and I'm a bit more integrated, I can sense on the spiritual level that I'm not completely well. I still fly into volatility when provoked.

A friend once told me, "My sickness is hoping I can make my husband sober by saying, 'If you really loved me you'd stop drinking.'" How I identify! Another confessed, "I can't help thinking that if he'd just try harder, he could pull himself up by his bootstraps and get on top of it." Once again, me too! Some convince themselves that if they just keep the house spotless, cook delicious meals, and dress up in sexy outfits when their husbands come home, all will be well. It's fine to want to be a supportive spouse, but we exhibit massive denial when we fantasize that we can seduce someone we love away from addiction. Such denial is our own illness.

Jesus tells us, "You will know the truth, and the truth will make you free" (John 8:32). The cure for denial comes in staring reality in the face and embracing the truth. Do we really want to get well? We'll know we do when we admit that addiction is, in fact, addiction. We'll know we do when we turn instinctively to Jesus in times of turbulence. We'll know we do when we make it a daily habit to pray seriously over scripture, asking the Holy Spirit to give us God's perspective on our loved one's struggles. We'll know we do when we begin to recognize our scary feelings, naming them and bringing them to the Lord. We'll know we do when we begin to practice the very things we wish our loved ones would do in order to get well themselves.

Prayer

Lord Jesus, help us see our own illness in the ways we deal with addicted loved ones, and give us the desire to get well. May we turn to scripture for wisdom and guidance. Give us courage to name our feelings and bring them to you. Put us in touch with caring friends, and give us fellowship with other believers. May we turn to you as the Great Physician on whom we can always rely. Amen.

17

Objectivity and Compassion

MATTHEW 12:15-21

*He will not break a bruised reed
or quench a smoldering wick
until he brings justice to victory.*

MANY CROWDS FOLLOWED him, and he cured all of them," Matthew tells us of Jesus, adding that he also warns them not to tell who he is. This warning is to fulfill the prophecy of Isaiah 42:1-4 concerning God's beloved Servant who will proclaim justice to the nations while keeping his own identity hidden, moving about quietly, careful neither to break a bruised reed nor snuff out a smoldering wick till he's brought justice to victory.

The tender image of not breaking a bruised reed juxtaposed against that grand mission statement—"until he brings justice to victory"—increases its poignancy. For Christians, Jesus embodies sensitive concern for the fragile and vulnerable, set against imagery suggesting a military march. In the American Southwest delicate flowers nestle between rocks, sheltered from the harsh heat and wind, all the more beautiful because they manage to survive in that terrain. This image of Jesus protecting the bruised reed "until he brings justice to victory" makes me think of those beautiful flowers.

The Bible provides this kind of contrast: a vast cosmic perspective set against the individual's vulnerability. It starts in Genesis with six magnificent grand-scale days of Creation, followed by an intimate close-up of Adam and Eve in the Garden as they play out the tragedy of the Fall. Throughout scripture, these two perspectives contrast with and complement each other, emphasizing God's grand sovereignty on the one hand and God's amazing compassion for vulnerable and sinful people on the other.

In our private lives, don't we need to maintain this delicate balance with our loved ones? What a challenge! It's hard to remain calm but firm as we insist on the danger of their behavior, while remaining sensitive to their brokenness and need. How many times I have failed to maintain this balance, lashing out in panic or frustration before I even realize what I've done! I know that incidents like this take a toll on my husband, just as his drinking takes a toll on me. I acknowledge that my failure to remain steady and calm indicates that I haven't dealt successfully with my own areas of addiction.

Even so, I try to remember that, just like my husband, I too am a bruised reed, a smoldering wick and that Jesus has compassion on me as well. I remember the Lord's encouragement in my own struggles, his strengthening me in self-control, and teaching me new ways of living fruitfully with my husband.

May all of us who struggle to maintain a delicate balance between tough objectivity and tender compassion look to the Lord for help, trusting in his unshakable love. Jesus probably has a thousand lessons still to teach us, lessons we have not as yet been ready to receive. Surely he will teach us these lessons when the time is right—when we have grown to the place where we can make good use of them.

Prayer

Lord Jesus, we thank you that you always met needy and vulnerable people with sensitivity and compassion, even as you set yourself like flint in your mission to bring justice to victory, ultimately going to the cross on our behalf. Thank you for the biblical balance between sovereignty and grace, between the sweep of salvation history and your great mercy toward the weak and vulnerable. Help us embody a similar balance in relationships with our loved ones. Amen.

18

Purity, the Core of Righteousness

MATTHEW 5:1-12

"Blessed are those who hunger and thirst for righteousness, for they will be filled."

"Blessed are the pure in heart, for they will see God."

W HEN JESUS SAW the crowds, he went up the mountain; and after he sat down, his disciples came to him. Then he began to speak, and taught them." So begins the introduction to the Sermon on the Mount. In his "Celebrate Recovery" (CR) ministry to alcoholics and other addicts, Pastor John Baker of Saddleback Church draws on the opening verses of this sermon, the much loved Beatitudes, as the spiritual foundation of CR's "Eight Principles." Indeed, the Beatitudes seem to describe an arc that may parallel the recovery journey.

How do the qualities Jesus blesses relate to the process of recovery? The poor in spirit are conscious of something missing in their souls; those who mourn have a similar awareness of loss that leaves them bereft; and those who are meek in the scriptural meaning of the word are humble and open to God's guidance. While the poor in spirit and those who mourn may sometimes experience a profound unspecified longing, in the fourth beatitude the hunger and thirst of the blessed ones becomes specific: they long for righteousness, a longing that only God's grace and membership in God's kingdom can satisfy. Significantly, the people Jesus blesses in the next three beatitudes—the merciful, the pure in heart, and the peacemakers—already embody attitudes of the heart that spring from the gift of the fourth beatitude, the gift of God's righteousness. Finally, with single-minded kingdom living we can expect persecution from powers that are in the world.

The purity of heart named in the sixth beatitude lies at the core of righteousness, for this quality protects us from deeper sins that Jesus addresses elsewhere in Matthew 5: adultery in the heart (v. 28) or murder committed spiritually if not literally when we hold on to anger (vv. 21-22). In my experience, purity of heart seems an elusive virtue as we guide the course of relationships with addicted loved ones. Our self-proclaimed desire to help, our ostensibly loving motives, often mask more complicated states of mind—pride, codependency, resentment—that reveal themselves as quite impure if we explore our feelings.

Introspection can be threatening. When we dig deep into what goes on in our hearts, we may unearth disturbing notions. We may discover that we have mixed feelings about whether we truly want an addicted loved one to find recovery! Sometimes the drama we know and live serves a perverse purpose for us, absorbing our attention so we don't have to face the fact that we ourselves need to change.

The late Elizabeth O'Connor, who published numerous books about the ecumenical Church of the Saviour in Washington, DC, wrote about "our many selves" in a book by the same name. There she offers quotations as food for contemplation, chosen to help readers recognize hidden feelings and motivations that exist side by side within so many of us. Exploring such impulses and urges can be a spiritual discipline, readying us to receive the gift of purity that comes only through the Holy Spirit.

It's a long and challenging journey. But if a part of us, on some level, truly hungers and thirsts for righteousness and for the purity of heart it brings, God will surely honor that longing.

Prayer

O God, grant that we may hunger and thirst for righteousness and for an ever greater intimacy with you. Grant also that in our relationships with addicted loved ones we may find increasing purity of heart so that we can bring a kingdom-of-heaven faith and vision to the challenges of these relationships. Give us the gifts of discernment and honesty as we examine our hearts and the courage to act on what we discover—one day at a time. Amen.

19

When We Struggle in Prayer

MATTHEW 6:5-13

"Pray then in this way."

SPEAKING TO HIS DISCIPLES in the Sermon on the Mount, Jesus teaches them to pray privately and in secret so that intimacy with their heavenly Father becomes their reward. Then they don't risk making their prayer a "show" for others. His thoughts on prayer go beyond this idea of whose approval we seek. He also counsels simplicity by stressing that the Father understands our needs and is eager to meet them. By giving us the Lord's Prayer, Jesus teaches us in a few short sentences to adore the Father, to intercede for God's kingdom so God's will may be done on earth as in heaven, to request material provision for today's needs, and to ask that our sins be forgiven as we forgive others so that we can be delivered from temptation and evil.

Some of us with addicted loved ones may find it hard to pray with the simplicity that Jesus counsels. I often find myself tied up in knots as I try to pray for my husband. Is it enough to ask for his sobriety? Should I pray for specific changes in his attitudes that seem to me necessary for recovery? Or is that somehow second-guessing God?

Even as I write this, I know intuitively that such introspective analysis isn't what God desires from us in prayer. Writing of his prep school days in *Surprised by Joy*, C. S. Lewis recalls his youthful self-examination attempts when he prayed. He found the practice so spiritually debilitating that he stopped praying altogether!

I often find it easier to bring complicated feelings to my husband than to bring them to Jesus! I remember one morning when my anguish came to a head. I broke down completely, telling Carl I was beginning to feel I should get in the car and leave, since I didn't seem to be doing either of us any good by staying. Hearing my own voice, I felt no "rightness" in my words; it felt as though I was being drawn into a terrible vortex pulling me down toward death and darkness, far away from God, my husband, and my own true self. Mercifully, my husband received my words with a gentle calm. As I wept it all out in his arms, my turbulence subsided, and I realized I didn't want to leave. Then I finally found peace.

What if I could cry out to God in the same way I cried out to my husband? What makes us feel that prayer must be perfect for God to receive our words? We have only to browse in the Psalms to see that God invites us to pray from the depths of our hearts, even when our feelings are turbulent and complicated.

What if Jesus taught us the Lord's Prayer as a standard to aim for and to encourage us to come to God in intimacy and trust? Some people enter the Lord's Prayer and make each verse their own as they pray it. For many of us drowning in feelings over a loved one's addiction, a single phrase from the Lord's Prayer can touch our hearts and help us spontaneously voice a core longing to God.

I experienced this sort of prayer on an evening shortly before my ninety-five-year-old father passed away. He had invited Jesus into his heart a few weeks before and, in those last months of his life, many decades of tension and misunderstanding between us were miraculously healed. As we prayed together, I asked Daddy if he ever tried to make the Lord's Prayer more personal to his situation. "Yes, I do," he replied. "I ask God to help me be a better father to you." Tears sprang to my eyes in that moment. Looking back on it now, I realize that my father, a lifelong agnostic till his mid-nineties, was showing me, his Christian daughter, how to pray.

Prayer

Thank you, Jesus, for teaching your disciples to pray with simplicity and faith. Relationships with our addicted loved ones sometimes leave us tied up in knots and make it hard for us to know what to pray for. Help us in our struggles, Lord, and teach us as you taught your disciples to pray, "Our Father in heaven, . . . Amen.

20

Self-Awareness and Obedience to the Lord

"Everyone then who hears these words of mine and acts on them will be like a wise man who built his house on rock."

THE ADVICE JESUS GIVES his listeners to build houses on rock consist of teachings in the Sermon on the Mount. Chapter 7 alone highlights so many: "Do not judge, so that you may not be judged" (v. 1); "Ask, and it will be given you" (v. 7); "Enter through the narrow gate" (v. 13). In chapters 5 and 6, other key quotes leap out—like those counseling us to store up treasures in heaven rather than on earth (6:19-20) and not worrying about tomorrow, "for tomorrow will bring worries of its own" (6:34).

Both this last command—not to worry about tomorrow—and the command to refrain from judging lest we be judged ourselves seem closely linked to principles in the recovery movement. I'm learning that beneath the judgmental thoughts that Jesus calls me to renounce, I also carry hidden anxiety that the Lord wants me to give over to him. My anxiety trips me up time and again, mak-

74   LOVING AN ADDICT

ing it hard for me never to worry about tomorrow and to approach life one day at a time. It's intriguing that I don't pay more prayerful attention to my tendency to worry because temperamentally it may be embedded in my nature just as much as my reflexive anger—another of my addictions.

Often our lives are ruled by feelings and thoughts that we don't even realize we have! A variation on this theme occurs when we think we are obeying a particular command, but our surface obedience masks unrecognized responses that violate another command. Consider, for example, Jesus' directive to turn the other cheek in Matthew 5:39. We've all known people who play the martyr in this fashion, while deep down they're holding on to self-righteous anger against the very ones over whom they fancy themselves so virtuous. Such behavior often arises in families contaminated by addiction.

Maybe one way to build our house on rock and to live more fully into all Jesus' teachings in the Sermon on the Mount is to ask Jesus to identify our camouflaged feelings and fears that drive us in our relationships with addicted loved ones. Counseling can help us develop self-awareness, as can honest conversation with trusted and trustworthy friends. If we reach out for help, we can surely grow in our capacity to put off the old self with its failings and to put on the new. As this happens, we will discover resource upon resource for greater wholeness in Jesus and for building our house on rock.

Prayer

Dear Lord, thank you for calling us to build our houses on rock by grounding ourselves in you as our only firm foundation. Show us, we pray, where our hidden feelings and anxieties unconsciously drive us. May we gain new integrity and grow into our new selves in you. Be our Rock when we feel storm-tossed by the turbulence of living with our loved ones. Keep us anchored in you—in your wisdom, love and grace. Amen.

21

Bringing Our Burdens to Jesus

MATTHEW 11:20-30

"Come to me, all you that are weary and are carrying heavy burdens, and I will give you rest."

THESE WORDS are some of the most comforting in the Gospels. How interesting, then, to realize that Jesus speaks them right after denouncing unrepentant cities where he has performed miracles—a significant context. Weariness and exhaustion, if you think about it, often presuppose oppressive circumstances. The flip side of compassion for pain can be wrath against the injustice that causes it.

Often in the families of addicts, children or wives shoulder the burden of responsibility: "If I just did a better job of being his wife. . . ."; "If I didn't do things that upset my dad. . . ." Some alcoholics in the throes of a drinking binge may hurl insults that reinforce feelings of responsibility and guilt.

To be sure, honesty demands that we acknowledge the sin in our own lives and take steps to deal with it. Let's never do this in a codependent spirit, though; let's never take on a burden of guilt for sin that isn't legitimately ours. The best approach we can take at the point of another's sin or addiction is to pray for that loved one's repentance and recovery in the same way we pray for our own.

Jesus understands the addict's struggles; he knows the spiritual, psychological, and physiological factors driving the addiction. How he must grieve over the intergenerational history of enslavement that underlies the situation! We can take heart that Jesus also understands all the ins and outs of the sinful responses to which we ourselves fall prey. The cue from this passage in Matthew's Gospel seems to be whether or not we and the addicts we love are sufficiently broken in spirit to surrender and repent. If so, we can imagine the rush of compassion coming from Jesus' heart and his eagerness to extend forgiveness.

Jesus longs for all of us to reach that place of brokenness where we come to the end of ourselves and accept the help he offers. We all feel weary and burdened by the compulsions that have us in their grip. Jesus desires to free every single one of us and bring us to rest in him.

PRAYER

Father God, we thank you that in his earthly life Jesus called the weary and burdened to come to him for rest, and we thank you that we can still find rest in you today. Help us never to buy into a loved one's accusation that his or her behavior is somehow our fault, even as you encourage us to recognize our own areas of sin. Bring us all to the place of brokenness that facilitates healing and restoration till we relinquish our burdens and find our rest in you. Amen.

22

The Gift of a Spiritual Family

MATTHEW 12:46-50

*"Whoever does the will of my Father in heaven
is my brother and sister and mother."*

As this Gospel passage opens, Jesus has just healed a demon-possessed man who was blind and mute. Now in the midst of the excited throng, the Pharisees try to undermine him by saying that he performs deliverances by the power of Beelzebul, the ruler of demons. This accusation sparks a lengthy and passionate response from Jesus. Mark's account tells us that Jesus' family has decided to "restrain him" because people say he is "out of his mind" (Mark 3:21)! So when Jesus asks who his mother and brothers are after someone mentions that his family is waiting outside, we can imagine the layers of complexity between the lines of the narrative. This time of intense pressure severely strains relational ties.

The nuclear family is not our only family, Jesus tells us here. Is it possible that in his view it's not even the most important? I think of an essay written by Richard Rohr, "Reflections on Marriage and Celibacy,"* in which he commented eloquently on this particular verse, stressing that Jesus' radical vision of family always encompasses the wider family of God and never limits itself to blood family alone. Family members wounded by addiction would do well to reflect on Jesus' provocative words in this passage. Sometimes when we feel overwhelmed by challenges with troubled family members, we need to seek a new perspective by immersing ourselves in alternate forms of family in the body of Christ—fellowship through groups in our church or visits with close and faithful friends.

Because I have no brothers, sisters, or children and my parents both passed away over a decade ago, I found it necessary in the years between divorce and remarriage to work intentionally to discover a spiritual family. I became involved in a church-based ministry to the homeless. After remarriage I withdrew from this ministry for a time, but then the morning came when I knew this had been a mistake. Putting issues of addiction on an emotional back burner, I headed over to the gathering place for the day's activities. I hadn't signed up—people certainly weren't expecting me—but it was like stepping into a different world. The excited embraces I received from folks who remembered me from previous years flooded my heart with new life. In my few but meaningful hours there, I felt Jesus' presence amid our gathering in a profound way. And that presence seemed to convey this thought: *Your work in this ministry is not over. Your marriage is not the only context for being with me, and it is not your only form of family. Remember that. Come and be with me here as well.*

I need you in this larger family of mine, and you need this family for yourself.

Upon returning home, I felt restored. I put the struggles of the previous night out of my mind, and my husband and I spent the rest of the day in harmony and peace. That temporary immersion in a family of Christian brothers and sisters, together with our beloved homeless guests, brought healing.

All of us with addicted loved ones need this understanding of a wider net of relationships—whether our struggles are with sons or daughters, siblings or parents, husbands or wives. Whatever the case, the Lord waits to replenish our hearts and give us new strength when we seek the restoring love of spiritual families. This type of fellowship nurtures and comforts us; our spiritual brothers and sisters challenge us to grow as their diverse gifts and experiences give us insights we could never have found on our own.

PRAYER

God, help us remember that in your realm, our true family consists of all who love and follow Jesus. Give us deep connections with this larger family when we have been wounded by troubles at home. Help us reach out for the love and care that we need; may we extend that same love and care to others inside and outside the body of Christ. Weave us together so that we are united in you by the power of the Holy Spirit. Amen.

Sojourners, 8, no. 5 (May 1979).

23

Tilling the Soil of Our Hearts

LUKE 8:4-8

"Let anyone with ears to hear listen!"

THIS CHALLENGING INVITATION comes as Jesus tells the parable of the sower and the seed, which all three synoptic Gospels report. The farmer scatters his seed abroad, and the way the plants do or do not thrive depends on where the seed lands. Does it fall on rocky soil, on soil choked by thorns? Is it simply trampled into the path by passersby? Or (in the best case scenario) does it fall on good ground and yield a rich crop?

We and the early hearers may have difficulty understanding Jesus' parables and wonder why he uses parables as a teaching tool. He explains to his disciples that he does this so that outsiders "'looking . . . may not perceive, and listening . . . may not understand'" (Luke 8:10). Doesn't he want his hearers to understand? The Isaiah passage that these words echo (Isaiah 6:9-10) may give a clue. In those verses God commands Isaiah to prophesy to the people so that hearing and seeing, they still won't understand. This divine instruction prompts Isaiah to ask how long this will continue. God replies, "Until cities lie waste without inhabitant, / and houses without people . . . / until the LORD sends everyone far away, / and vast is the emptiness in the midst of the land" (6:11-12)—in other words, until the Babylonian exile. God's words suggest that ignorance will not remain forever and ultimately people will be ready to hear, to see, and to understand.

The implications of this passage in Isaiah call to mind a basic principle of recovery dynamics. Just as addicts must experience a kind of bottoming out before they can fruitfully integrate recovery insights into their lives and just as premature conceptual understanding may be worse than useless, so events in Jesus' day also may have needed to run their course. Only then would the ultimate outcome unfold according to God's sovereign will. Jesus understood that the powers that be and many of the people were not yet ready to receive his teachings. The learning required some experiential lessons. Perhaps for this reason he scattered his message abroad far and wide, hiding it in poetry, metaphor, and parables, much as the farmer in this parable scatters the seed. If by the grace of God it happens to land on good soil where it could take strong root and multiply that would be a blessing. But if not—if the soil was not yet ready to nourish the seed into fruitful growth—then so be it.

What does this parable mean for those of us who have addicted loved ones? We can't know when or how God will bring them to recovery. We certainly can't control it ourselves. We can ask the Holy Spirit to till the soil of our own hearts as we pray, immerse ourselves in scripture, and build relationships of trust and vulnerability with loyal Christian friends. Then, perhaps, the seeds Jesus scatters into our lives can begin to take solid root and produce some of the fruit described in Galatians 5—love, joy, peace, patience, kindness, generosity, faithfulness, gentleness, and self-control.

We may not be anywhere near this point in our Christian growth. Thorns of worry, shame, or anger may choke the soil of our hearts; the hard circumstances we face may trample underfoot the seeds of Jesus' words. In time, as we continue to ask the Holy Spirit to till the soil of our hearts, we will grow to greater fruitfulness.

Prayer

Thank you, loving God, for adopting us as children into your family of faith. How we long for greater fruitfulness in you and a deeper life of discipleship! Help us realize that just as the farmer can't predict how, where, or when the scattered seed will germinate and bear fruit, so we can't predict or control how your healing word will bear fruit in our lives and in the lives of those we love. Help us to trust that you will bring about the fruit-bearing in your own way and in your own time. Amen.

24

Faith in the Midst of the Storm

MATTHEW 8:18, 23-27

"Why are you afraid, you of little faith?"

JESUS AND HIS DISCIPLES are in a boat, crossing to the other side of the lake. A great storm arises over the water and the waves crash into the boat, breaking over the side and nearly swamping the terrified disciples. Jesus himself remains totally oblivious to the danger; in fact, he sleeps! The disciples waken him, begging him to save them. Doesn't he care that they are about to drown? On waking and looking around at the extent of the storm, he merely asks, "Why are you afraid, you of little faith?" Then he rises and rebukes the wind and the waves. Suddenly the water becomes completely calm!

I appreciate this passage because a longtime friend who was doing missionary work in Indonesia had a similar experience. He was taking some people by boat to a prayer gathering at a little island when such a storm arose. His companions were terrified, but my friend remained peaceful. Bewildered by his composure, the others demanded to know why he wasn't scared. My friend Irving laughed and replied, grinning, "Because Jesus is in the boat!"

My friend's radical faith and intimate relationship with the Lord led him to testify to his experience. Many of us lack a hardy faith. When we encounter stormy seas—figurative as well as literal—how do we respond? I can recall the gathering storms at home when I have riled up the waters by my own agitation instead of detaching from anxious involvement and trusting Jesus to take control of the situation.

Once in a great while, I have attempted to respond in a new way: I have stayed calm and pulled back from destructive entanglement. Once or twice I have spoken the truth in love, knowing that Jesus, through the Holy Spirit, had calmed a potential storm in my heart. Finally, God has often brought me to the point—if not in the actual moment of crisis, then at least shortly afterward—where I find myself remembering and giving thanks for my husband's many fine qualities, the ways that he loves the Lord and lives out biblical principles in areas of his life that don't involve alcohol.

But a word of caution here: When we have breakthroughs like this in our own responses, we cannot assume that we will never relapse into stormy emotions again. It's also important not to expect instant results in the form of changed behavior on the part of addicted loved ones.

Instead, we give thanks for the grace of each new breakthrough, all the while praying for our ongoing stability, as well as for the recovery of those we love. Though we can't possibly know when or if full recovery will be granted this side of heaven, resting in gratitude for the blessings of the present moment will work wonders for our spirits. For now, the increasing peace we sometimes experience in our own hearts needs to be our reward. As we begin to grow into faith, hope, and love, we increasingly know that in our own storm Jesus will be in the boat.

PRAYER

Lord, we can only imagine the terror of those disciples as the storm swept over them at sea, threatening to swamp the boat that carried them. Thank you for faithful and gifted followers who remain at peace when chaos overtakes their lives. Increase our faith so that we too may come to know the peace that passes understanding when the storms of life threaten to overwhelm us. May we abandon our own agendas, leaving our loved ones in your hands and trusting in your love. Amen.

25

When Wisdom Meets Innocence

MATTHEW 10:1, 5-16

"Be wise as serpents and innocent as doves."

Jesus prepares his disciples to head out on a mission, and he does so by radically upping the ante on what will be required of them. He warns them of dangers they will encounter, emphasizing that they will have to depend on faith alone. They will be sheep among wolves; they must be as wise as serpents and as innocent as doves. Divisions between those who do and do not respond will become more dramatic now. Despite inevitable persecution, they are not to fear.

Jesus' words here echo his teaching in the Sermon on the Mount, especially in Matthew 6:25-34 with its challenges not to worry about tomorrow but simply to trust in God. Ordinary human concerns pale in significance when set against the call to live into God's kingdom—not just in the hereafter but every day in the earthly here and now.

The challenging call may resonate in our hearts, even as more timid parts of us hold back and resist. Are others with addicted loved ones conscious, as I am, of these conflicting impulses and urges? Sometimes we long to embrace a greater kingdom living that seems impossible, given the constraints of our personal circumstances. Sometimes we may want to retreat. Either way, we dare not sink into paralysis over the obstacles and confusions in our lives or lose faith in God's capacity to bring us to new breakthroughs. We accept responsibility for discovering our present call from God today as best we understand it.

Speaking for myself, I currently sense that the Lord wants me to learn how to be wise as a serpent and innocent as a dove in the context of this marriage: to be unflinchingly honest about what's going on; to sharpen my objectivity by drawing on every bit of discernment, common sense, and clinical insight available, all the while praying to embody love, patience, gentleness, self-control, and the other fruit of the Spirit listed in Galatians 5. I believe the Lord wants me to accept my husband fully and to love him unconditionally—not in the sense of believing that everything he does is acceptable but rather in the sense of taking a clear-eyed look at exactly who he is and how he struggles, even as I strive to embody understanding, compassion, and love. What a challenge! While these Gospel reflections have helped me grow in my ability to love in this way, all too often I fail and fall back into old patterns.

Biblical images of marriage, together with our own hopes and dreams, may lure us with idealistic visions of instant intimacy and perfect Christian partnership. In our wiser moments, we acknowledge that we can't merge with our spouses in the way scripture often depicts. A healthy and loving detachment seems necessary—not only for our psychological survival but for our spiritual health as well, and ultimately for the spiritual health of the union. With addicted loved ones other than our spouses—parents, sons, daughters, brothers, or sisters—we also need to practice loving with this kind of caring detachment that allows us to communicate clearly and camly.

Prayer

God, may we be "wise as serpents and innocent as doves" as we face the challenges in our lives. Help us develop a tough love even as we embody love, patience, gentleness, and self-control. We know, Lord, that without your grace we can do none of this. So be with us, and help us to trust in your presence. Amen.

26

Crying Out for Help

MATTHEW 14:22-33

*When [Peter] noticed the strong wind, he became
frightened, and beginning to sink,
he cried out, "Lord, save me!"*

IN THE DRAMATIC MOMENT captured here, Peter faces
a major test of faith. The disciples have just witnessed the
miraculous feeding of the five thousand, where Jesus mul-
tiplied five loaves of bread and two fish to feed a hungry
multitude. With everyone fed and satisfied, Jesus has urged
his disciples into a boat to start their journey to the other
side of the lake so that he can go off by himself to pray. So
here the disciples are in the boat again. Suddenly—amazingly—they see Jesus coming toward them, walking on the
water. We can imagine that impetuous Peter, all charged
up by his recent experiences of Jesus' power, would indeed
call out, "Lord, if it is you, command me to come to you
on the water." His courage lasts only a moment. Once he
steps out on the surface of the sea, he feels the wind and
suddenly panics. Beginning to sink, he cries out for Jesus
to save him.

We can easily read this account metaphorically as a description of an addict's struggles in recovery—managing to stay sober or clean for a time, only to relapse once again when crisis or temptation strikes. "Lord, save me!" is a cry that many addicts instinctively utter many times. But isn't this cry also on the lips and in the hearts of those of us who love them? When we give in to our own addiction to anger, worry, or despair by taking one or two steps forward only to fall back again, this story can offer comfort.

To begin with, we need to realize that growth does indeed occur. No longer terrified as in the earlier boat trip, Peter now steps out in faith and begins to walk on the water. But of course his attention shifts from Jesus to the wind and the waves, proving as he starts to sink that his newfound confidence is short-lived. But for a moment, he had it! I find this image of real if bumpy growth encouraging, even as I confess that reading of Peter's "relapse" reassures me that I'm not alone when I yield repeatedly to weakness. Most comforting of all is the knowledge that Jesus understands. "You of little faith, why did you doubt?" Jesus asks. But immediately he reaches out, takes Peter's hand, and pulls him up from the water.

Our own relapses may be less dramatic than Peter's! However, we may feel discouraged when we revert to the same patterns time and again when triggered by a loved one's behavior. But what if God allows repeated relapses to provide opportunities for fresh insight and time to discover buried feelings, like pain we haven't wanted to face?

Don't we all carry profound sadness over the contrast between the person we know our addicted loved one has the potential to be, and the person he or she becomes in the throes of addicted behavior? Speaking for myself, when I break through my anger and touch into this grief, healing tears begin to flow and prayers I can't pray when I'm trapped in resentment come pouring out of my soul.

During such times I know that, like Peter, I am on a faith journey that leads me into new growth. If periodically we take our eyes off Jesus and fall back into churning waters of codependency and turmoil, shame and fear, such relapses won't become the last word of the story. Jesus will be there to reassure us. He will reach out his hand to rescue us and help us back into the boat.

Prayer

Lord, as we grow in our relationship with you, we know we will face periods of testing, and sometimes our faith will falter. Still, as we move into riskier waters, may we understand more fully all that is hidden in our hearts—grief we haven't wanted to face, anxieties we didn't realize we had. Then, when we cry out to you, "Lord, save us!" reach out your hand and catch us. Amen.

27

The Gift of an Eternal Perspective

JOHN 6:22-29

*"You are looking for me . . . because
you ate your fill of the loaves."*

THE CROWDS FOLLOWING Jesus realize he has vanished after miraculously multiplying the loaves and fishes to feed five thousand people, but they can't figure out where he has gone. So some of those who witnessed the miracle climb into boats and head to the other side of the lake at Capernaum in search of him. Finding him there, they ask him when he arrived. Jesus lets them know that he understands they are searching for him not because they witnessed and responded to a divine sign but because that miracle happened to satisfy their physical hunger. Then he adds, "Do not work for the food that perishes, but for the food that endures for eternal life, which the Son of Man will give you. . . . This is the work of God, that you believe in him whom he has sent."

Many of us may have experienced the difference between seeking Jesus simply to eat our fill of the loaves versus seeking him out of a genuine desire for "food that endures for eternal life." I remember such a moment of recognition many years ago, soon after suffering the pain of divorce, and long before meeting my present husband. Jesus' love had broken over me in amazing ways during the months my husband was leaving our marriage. Those experiences filled me with awe and invited me to immerse myself in the Gospel narratives that brought Jesus vividly to life. Yet given my broken and needy condition, I perceived that I cared more to find healing and comfort from Jesus than to seek him as Lord and embrace his radical claims on my life.

One weekend, during a time of aching loneliness, I traveled to a seaside cottage for a few days of retreat. The first night I went to bed in a state of despair. When I awoke the next morning, impressions of joy greeted my senses. The sky was a radiant and cloudless blue; the wind chimes outside sounded idyllic, blending with the distant cry of gulls. Taking a cup of coffee out to the deck, I impulsively picked up my Bible and opened it at random (or so I thought) to this passage in John 6. As I read Jesus' words—"Very truly, I tell you, you are looking for me, not because you saw signs, but because you ate your fill of the loaves. . . . This is the work of God, that you believe in him whom he has sent"—tears sprang to my eyes, and I felt a kaleidoscopic shift in my heart. I felt as if Jesus stood right there, speaking directly to me. His challenging words brought healing, for the challenge was offered in love.

Have I focused primarily, since then, on the food that endures to eternal life? Have I believed perfectly since then? No, of course I haven't. To do that I would have to transcend discouragement over issues of addiction. I would have to believe deep down that whatever the outward circumstances, God is working out a sovereign purpose in our lives despite my failure to understand it. And I don't believe this all the time, though occasionally I feel its truth in my heart. I feel this truth more often and more strongly since I've been meeting Jesus in the Gospel narratives. Reflecting on how these stories touch me personally, I've been tapping into a powerful healing resource. I have been giving thanks for Carl's strong qualities that so enrich our life together when he's not drinking and building on this gratitude to shore up my faith. As this happens, I'm discovering an eternal perspective, looking beyond food that perishes and seeking food that endures for eternal life.

Prayer

God of life, you know our vulnerability to the lures of the world—the expectations and assumptions that distract us from you. As we live with addicted loved ones, free us from thinking that the only thing we need is their instant healing. We know that you want us to pray for their healing, but even more than this you want them—and us—to find our true selves in a deeper relationship with you. May we discover that you are the Bread of Life for our souls, and grant us an eternal perspective so we can affirm this truth in our hearts. Amen.

28

The Blessing of Jesus' Humanity

MARK 7:31-37

Then looking up to heaven, [Jesus] sighed and said to him, "Ephphatha," that is, "Be opened."

JESUS HAS GONE to the Sea of Galilee, and people bring him a deaf mute who desires healing. Jesus leads the man a distance away from the crowd, puts his fingers into his ear, spits, and touches his tongue. And immediately, on command, the deaf mute is healed. Jesus tells the onlookers to keep it quiet, but of course they ignore him and begin to spread the news abroad.

The verse describing Jesus' deep sigh opens a window onto Jesus' humanness! What lies behind that deep sigh? Almost certainly he experiences exhaustion with the overwhelming number of folks flocking to him and the vast extent of their sickness and suffering. The sigh may surface over his own disciples' constant failure to demonstrate the faith needed to cure and possibly over his own emotional isolation and human loneliness. No one seems to understand who Jesus is, much less his purpose and mission. The disciples are so dense; the crowds so focused on their own neediness. The frustration that occasionally erupts from Jesus when the disciples fail to get his teaching or to demonstrate the power to heal testifies to this exhaustion.

We may feel uncomfortable concentrating on Jesus' human vulnerability. We may not feel inspired to take this all-too-earthly Jesus into our hearts, caught as he is in the constraints of Incarnation. Some of us may prefer the glorified risen Christ.

Others may resonate with Jesus' humanness. When I was first coming to faith decades ago, my heart went out to this very human Jesus as I encountered him in the Gospel narratives! I had little faith in his resurrection; perhaps, I thought, he really had died once and for all on that cross. My heart broke to think of what he must have gone through in the agony of his physical suffering, the intensity of his feeling abandoned by God. But my imaginative connection with Jesus in those days fueled my prayer life. Looking back on that time from the perspective of my current more mature faith, I find myself affirming the importance of revisiting and reflecting on this human Jesus as portrayed in the Bible.

Jesus emphasizes his radical identification with the vulnerable and suffering. His words in Matthew 25 tell us that whenever we minister to the hungry, the poor and needy, the sick, the prisoner, we minister to him. Just as God came to us in Jesus, so Jesus now comes to us in the broken and needy ones we encounter in our lives, in those around us bowed down with exhaustion and discouragement. Seeing them, he wants us to see him.

Is it too much to suggest that Jesus also wants us to see him in our troubled loved ones and to practice loving him with a deeper and more sacrificial love as we learn how better to love them? How different would our response to those loved ones be if we could begin to recognize Jesus in their humanness, their brokenness, and their need?

And when exhaustion and discouragement overcome us, it is good to recognize him in ourselves also.

Prayer

Lord, we worship you in gratitude and awe for your redemptive death on the cross. Help us cherish the gift of your embodied life and ministry. As we realize how often you experienced exhaustion yet continually poured yourself out for the needy, give us a glimpse of the paradoxical sacredness of your own vulnerability. Help us see you in the struggles of our loved ones and in our own struggles as well. Amen.

29

Pain as the Training Ground for Discipleship

MARK 8:27-35

"Who do you say that I am?"

JOURNEYING TO CAESAREA PHILIPPI, Jesus asks his disciples, "Who do people say that I am?" When they reply that some say he is John the Baptist or Elijah or another of the prophets, he asks a critical second question: "But who do you say that I am?" Without hesitation, Peter responds, "You are the Messiah." Immediately Jesus warns them not to tell anyone and proceeds to instruct them on everything he must suffer in the near future, including crucifixion, before being raised from the dead. Peter, the very one who has just made that great declaration of faith, protests in horror, but Jesus rebukes him for addressing "human things." Calling the crowds, Jesus begins to spell out the radical cost of discipleship: "Those who want to save their life will lose it, and those who lose their life for my sake, and for the sake of the gospel, will save it."

This sharp turning point in the Gospel narrative initiates a time of greater demand on the disciples. Jesus has intimated the cost of discipleship when he sends them out on mission, but now we sense a relentless drive in the narrative. From this point on, we are heading toward Jerusalem: toward crucifixion for Jesus and toward testing for the disciples—and for us.

"Who do you say that I am?" That Peter initially gives an inspired response to that question, only to give way in the next moment to a worldly perspective, instinctively choosing safety and comfort above God's call, may feel disturbingly familiar. When I respond to my husband's drinking more in terms of the pain it causes me than out of concern for his welfare, I am succumbing to an unconscious sense of entitlement. I react as though my life should be cushy and comfortable—never mind the suffering I see all around me. I am, like Peter, horrified by the cross.

I'm not alone in this resistance. It's one thing to want to be with Jesus when we're experiencing consolation and healing power. It's quite another to desire intimacy with the Lord when he's calling us to accompany him on a journey bound to involve suffering, sacrifice, and pain. But pain can serve as a training ground for discipleship. In my case, my marriage throws into bold relief my desire to control my circumstances, even though I know that I can't! It exposes my emotional volatility and forces me to turn to Jesus for self-control in times of stress. Who do I say Jesus is? If he is my Lord, then surely he has a right to ask anything he wants of me and to use hard circumstances to shape me into the person he would have me become.

Doesn't this principle hold true in the lives of all who struggle with the behavior of addicted loved ones? We may find it fruitful to ask ourselves and to ask God what in our circumstances provides the opportunity to grow into deeper discipleship. If we truly believe Jesus is Lord, we can welcome the breaking down of our defenses so that we can open ourselves more fully to him. Do we mean what we say when we call him Lord? Deep in our hearts, who do we say Jesus is?

PRAYER

Help us understand, Jesus, that if we see you as Lord, we can expect challenges that allow us to grow in discipleship. We confess we have no right to expect healing of our loved ones as a special gift to us. Lord, help us rethink our assumptions so that we can, in your servant Paul's words, be transformed by the renewing of our minds and take every thought captive to obey you. Lead us to consider whether we simply call you Lord or actually believe that you are. Amen.

30

Listening to the Lord

Mark 9:2-8

"This is my Son, the Beloved; listen to him!"

Shortly after Peter's inspired confession of faith at Caesarea Philippi, Jesus takes him, along with James and John, to the top of a high mountain. There Jesus is transfigured before their eyes. His clothes shine dazzling white, and the disciples watch astounded as Moses and Elijah appear and stand there talking with Jesus. Terrified, Peter babbles an irrelevant suggestion that they erect three shelters to commemorate the event, whereupon a cloud envelops them; they hear God's voice say, "This is my Son, the Beloved; listen to him!" Immediately as they look around, they see no one except Jesus.

"Listen to him." How often does Jesus speak to us and in what ways? How closely are we listening? Are we listening more closely today than when we first came to faith? Or are we sometimes listening less? I know that this can be said of me.

My first encounter with Jesus' amazing love came over two decades ago, when my first marriage was crumbling. Though I was an agnostic at the time, one afternoon I knelt down beside our bed, weeping, and heard myself cry out almost involuntarily, "Jesus, please help me." In the wake of that prayer a peace flooded over me that did pass all understanding. In the months that followed that awesome experience, the fabric of my life continued its relentless unraveling. My heart broke as my husband decided to leave our home and our marriage. Yet spiritually I experienced this time as one of great blessing. Immersing myself in the Bible day after day and late into the night, several translations of scripture and dozens of theological commentaries piled all over the desk, I had one goal in mind: to learn to listen to Jesus.

One night a frightening thought hit me: *Aren't you afraid of going crazy, shutting yourself up all alone like this with all these books, night after night after night?* In response, I heard a reassuring voice with the ears of my heart: *Keep focusing on me in those Gospel stories. Pay attention to my effect on people, the way I healed them and brought them to new wholeness. You have nothing to fear if you're centered in me. Just keep listening.* Gradually, as I listened to the many different "voices" I heard, I learned to distinguish between the whispered words of the Holy Spirit and the thoughts that reflected my anxious fears. I came to understand that the Holy Spirit would always point me to the Bible and make Jesus' voice alive to me.

Dramatic experiences of hearing Jesus' voice came to me decades ago when I stood at the brink of personal disintegration. Surrender came easily at that time—I had no other choice. Then, during subsequent years of single-again living, I practiced taking charge of my life. I came to enjoy the feeling of personal freedom and began to relish autonomous living. That is why praying through these Gospel reflections is so critical. They become my antidote when instinctively I listen to self rather than to Jesus.

By abandoning ourselves to him a little more each day and by immersing ourselves in the Gospel narratives that let us listen in on his conversations, we can learn to recognize his voice and understand what he is trying to say to each one of us, here and now, in our unique struggles with the ones we love. What will I hear Jesus say to me today if I surrender my need for control? What will each of us hear?

Prayer

Help us recognize, Lord Jesus, that if we truly want to hear your voice, we can only do so in a spirit of humility and vulnerability. May we realize that our suffering, particularly with addicted loved ones, offers an opportunity to hear your voice afresh. Inspire us to let go of our need to control and of any denial about our circumstances. Give us the wisdom to realize that your perspective far exceeds our own and that your dreams for us exceed whatever we can imagine. Amen.

31

The Courage to Surrender in Prayer

MARK 9:14-29

"I believe; help my unbelief!"

JESUS, PETER, JAMES, AND JOHN have come down from the mountain where the three disciples witnessed the miracle of the Transfiguration and saw Jesus resplendent in white, standing together with Moses and Elijah. On coming back "down to earth," they find a large crowd gathered around a man and his demon-possessed son. Jesus' disciples, the man explains, were unable to heal the boy, and he implores Jesus to help them—"if you are able." "If you are able!" Jesus exclaims. "All things can be done for the one who believes." Immediately the boy's father cries out, "I believe; help my unbelief!"

The theme of belief or the lack of it infuses this passage. "You faithless generation, how much longer must I be among you?" Jesus exclaims in frustration. Yet as soon as the man begs for help and blurts out his ambivalent confession of faith—"I believe; help my unbelief"—Jesus' exasperation seems to pass. He simply rolls up his sleeves and goes to work, casting out the spirit that has made the boy mute.

What does it mean to believe in Jesus? Reverend Tim Keller, pastor of New York City's Redeemer Presbyterian Church, gave an intriguing sermon titled "John Meets Jesus" (4/27/97), in which he noted that whenever we read the phrase "belief in Jesus" in John's Gospel, the original Greek (which always uses the preposition "eis") might more accurately be translated as "belief into Jesus." What might it mean to "believe into" Jesus rather than simply "believe in" him? Keller suggests that "believing in" merely involves intellectual assent, while "believing into" involves the faith and trust that enables persons to follow even when danger threatens.

Simply praying for healing, which Jesus clearly commands, involves taking a risk: *What if God doesn't answer our prayers according to our wishes?* Often I cling to so many hopes and expectations about how (and when) I want my prayers answered that I cannot pray with abandon.

Here's the bottom-line question: Am I beginning to doubt that Jesus can heal both my husband's drinking problem and my addiction to emotional turbulence? No, I believe Jesus can do that. But what does feel hard is believing "into" Jesus for this healing, praying in a spirit of absolute trust and surrender.

New questions arise: What if we could relinquish our own agendas? What if we were to turn from specific prayer requests and commit our loved ones and ourselves into the Lord's sovereign care? What if we ask the Holy Spirit to deepen our faith so that God will orchestrate unfolding events in our lives in the best possible way—and then leave it at that?

Do we dare to trust God this deeply when we're bowed down by the ache of a loved one's addiction and discouraged by our responses? Can we confidently place our faith in the promise of Romans 8:28, believing that God will bring ultimate good out of our circumstances if we seek to embrace the Lord's call on our lives as best we understand it?

Searching my heart again now, I know that on one level I do trust God in this way. But if I'm absolutely honest, I have to admit that a trace of doubt remains. Intuitively then I must cry, along with the grieving father in the Gospel story, "I believe; help my unbelief!"

PRAYER

Lord God, we confess that we're clinging to our own expectations and agendas when it comes to praying for our loved ones' healing. Release us from the need to control. Give us the gift of a stronger faith in your sovereignty and mercy. Lord, we do believe. Help our unbelief. Amen.

32

Forgiveness and the Heart of Prayer

MATTHEW 18:19-22

"Not seven times, but, I tell you, seventy-seven times."

PETER, ALWAYS THE EAGER ONE and no doubt imagining that Jesus is suggesting radical forgiveness, asks him this question: "Lord, if another member of the church sins against me, how often should I forgive? As many as seven times?" (v. 21). Jesus' reply probably startles him: "Not seven times, but, I tell you, seventy-seven times." A few verses earlier, Jesus has promised that when two believers remain in agreement as they pray together, his Father in heaven will grant their request; similarly, when two or three gather in his name, he will be with them. Reading between the lines, I wonder if agreeing in prayer and standing together in Jesus' name may mean more than just seeing eye to eye on the content of the request.

What if Jesus' words imply that true agreement in prayer means being united in a spirit of humility, restoration, and reconciliation wherever there has been a rift? What if it means a readiness to forgive one another not seven times but seventy-seven times? These conditions establish the groundwork for powerful shared prayer.

My husband and I pray together daily. But how often do we unite in the way Jesus describes here? Let me speak for myself. What goes on in my heart? Have I ever subconsciously thought, *Surely I've forgiven enough already—for now?* How ungrateful and ironic that attitude would be, given that my husband consistently forgives my strong feelings toward him and his behavior! Nevertheless, "the heart is devious above all else" (Jer. 17:9). Do I really know everything that's hidden in my own heart?

If I'm harboring an unconscious lack of forgiveness when my husband and I come together to pray, that would skew my heart away from the reconciling spirit that Jesus suggests as foundational for effective prayer. If I'm resenting the ways I feel my husband has hurt me, I can safely assume that I'm failing to recognize the many ways I have hurt him.

There's something about substance abuse that can seduce us into distorted thinking. We can easily focus on the addictive behavior as though it were a special kind of sin that trumps any of our own. Don't we occasionally hold fast to the notion that because we are sober or clean that we are a notch above our loved ones at the point of moral merit?

Until we recognize and renounce such hidden attitudes, we can scarcely understand the sinfulness involved in our own responses or remember to give thanks for the positive qualities we often ignore in the addicts whom we love. Even more, there's little chance we'll be able to understand our addiction to our own dysfunctional behaviors. We need to face the unvarnished truth without protective blinders, resting in the vast expanse of Jesus' limitless forgiveness for the many ways—intentional and unintentional—we have hurt our loved ones and thus have also hurt him. This realization better positions us to let the Lord change our hearts so we can begin to forgive seventy-seven times. Then perhaps we will pray with real power.

Prayer

Thank you, Father, for Jesus' challenging words. Thank you for the assurance that when we gather in agreement as we pray, you will grant our request. We are overwhelmed by Jesus' promise that when two or three gather in his name, he is with them. Help us to find partners in prayer and then encourage us to pray with real power and cleansed, forgiving hearts. Amen.

33

Our Loved Ones as Neighbors

LUKE 10:25-37

"Which of these three, do you think, was a neighbor?"

A LAWYER, SEEKING TO TEST Jesus, inquires what he must do to inherit this "eternal life" about which Jesus is speaking. Turning the question back to him, Jesus asks what the law says, and the man replies, "You shall love the Lord your God with all your heart, and with all your soul, and with all your strength, and with all your mind; and your neighbor as yourself." Jesus commends him for his reply, telling him that if he obeys this command, he will live. The lawyer wants to justify himself, however, so he tries to narrow that enormous challenge to a more comfortable legalism. "And who," he asks, "is my neighbor?" He must get a rude shock when Jesus, refusing to appease him, instead tells the familiar story of the man beaten and nearly killed by robbers. He is rescued by an outsider—a Samaritan—after a priest and Levite have passed by on the other side of the road. Jesus then asks a provocative question: "Which of these three, do you think, was a neighbor to the man who fell into the hands of the robbers?"

Jesus refuses to let the lawyer off the hook by giving him a tidy category of people the lawyer may appropriately deem as neighbors. Instead, he implies that entering the realm of kingdom living involves a radical identity shift. In that kingdom realm we become neighbors to any and all who cross our path.

So many experiences over the years have taught me that the more we center on this question and try to become neighbors in our relationships, the more Jesus can work in our hearts to free us and heal us. For those of us living with alcoholics or other addicts, the call to become a neighbor carries special meaning close to home. Neighbor love is grounded in the compassion and concern with which Jesus loves us and which God can plant in our hearts when we ask for it. This love doesn't depend on personal gratification from the other to survive and flourish; rather, the love we have received from God nurtures neighbor love (1 John 4:19). What if Jesus is calling us to extend this kind of neighbor love to our addicted loved ones when we are grieved, frightened, or angry at the ways their behavior is wounding us? What if he is calling us to meet them with a generous tough love grounded in honesty, self-discipline, and compassion?

If we confess how hard it is for us to do this and honestly seek Jesus' help, surely the Holy Spirit will empower us to love them in this agape fashion. In the process we will learn to value ourselves and our loved ones as God values us and them; we desire to become the women and men

God wants us to be. More significantly, we will appreciate anew the truth that we ourselves can only hope to love in this way "because he first loved us" (1 John 4:19).

So we bring all our pain and weakness to the Lord. We reach out to our Christian sisters and brothers and let them minister to us in our exhaustion, sorrow, discouragement, and grief. As we reflect on Jesus' parable about being a neighbor, we need to identify with the wounded one by the side of the road as well as with the Samaritan who stoops to help him.

PRAYER

God of love, thank you that we don't need to rely on our own resources when it comes to loving our neighbors but that we love because you first loved us. Help us truly long for a change of heart so we can begin to see struggling loved ones not only as intimates who cause us pain but as neighbors whom you call us to love. May we discover our true self-worth in you. Amen.

34

Sitting at Jesus' Feet

LUKE 10:38-42

"There is need of only one thing."

IMMEDIATELY AFTER THE PARABLE of the good Samaritan we read the story of Mary and Martha. Jesus goes to their home, where he finds Martha distracted with serving, while her sister Mary sits at his feet and listens to his teaching. Martha rebukes Mary for not helping with the tasks of hostessing, but Jesus turns the rebuke around. "Martha, Martha, you are worried and distracted by many things; there is need of only one thing. Mary has chosen the better part, which will not be taken away from her."

When we try to practice compassionate concern in our own lives, especially with addicted loved ones, often our emotions rise up defiantly, clamoring for attention and distracting us from approaching those loved ones as neighbors. A hundred outer demands—responsibilities with work, household tasks, or other relationships—wind up unsettling us also. Yet by placing the parable of the good Samaritan and the story of the Mary-Martha encounter back to back, the Gospel of Luke implies that as we practice agape love with others, we are to look to Mary as our example—contemplative, passive Mary, sitting at Jesus' feet and drinking in his words. We ready ourselves for service in the peaceful, receptive spirit of Mary. Now there's a challenge!

A personal memory comes to mind. About a decade ago I cared for my elderly father. I visited him several times a day in a care facility while juggling other responsibilities. I would hurry through the depressing corridor to his room at the end of the hall, passing folks in wheelchairs who lined the wall and giving each a cursory greeting as I sped by. Then one day something clicked inside me. I began to pause (it only took a second) to meet each person's eyes and to open myself to a tiny but genuine encounter with each one. I couldn't believe it! It felt so different, and I could see the difference it made to them. *Is this the way you have been wanting me to interact all along?* I silently asked Jesus. And in my heart I heard him answer yes.

Can we learn to be with our loved ones at potentially tempestuous times in this surrendered spirit, listening to Jesus rather than to all the emotions inside us that clamor for expression?

One thing is sure. If we want to face our challenges in the contemplative spirit of Mary, we will place God first in our lives. We practice shifting our attention from the inner emotional turmoil to the awareness of Jesus' presence with us. We turn consciously from the streams of thought and emotion that have been agitating us to intentionally focusing on Jesus. I made this choice the other day, and for a moment I found myself in a different realm: one of steadiness, spaciousness, and peace.

Victories like this are few and far between in my experience. But without a doubt these scriptural reflections have been changing my heart little by little and readying my spirit for the breakthrough that particular day. How exciting it feels to get imaginatively and spiritually closer to Jesus through the Gospel narratives! By immersing ourselves in these passages we sit at his feet like Mary, basking in his words.

Prayer

Dear Lord, help us sense what it could mean to see neighbor love as a response that springs naturally from our hearts when we make it a habit to sit at your feet, drinking in your words. May we long for the peace such love can bring into our lives and the lives of others. May we turn to you and listen for your voice in all our encounters with addicted loved ones. We need your help to demonstrate neighbor love to them through the power of the Holy Spirit. Amen.

35

Radical Grace in God's Kingdom

LUKE 13:10-21

"What is the kingdom of God like?"

WHAT IS THE KINGDOM OF GOD LIKE?" Jesus asks, as the leader of the synagogue and a crowd of religious leaders and bystanders look on. It is the sabbath, and Jesus has broken Jewish law by healing a woman crippled for eighteen long years by a spirit, a woman now released from her bondage and joyfully praising God. The leader of the synagogue isn't impressed. Angry at Jesus but apparently reluctant to challenge him directly, he instead lays a guilt trip on the one who has just been healed and rebukes her for seeking healing on the sabbath. "You hypocrites!" Jesus declares. "Does not each of you on the sabbath untie his ox or his donkey . . . ? And ought not this woman . . . be set free from this bondage on the sabbath day?"

"What is the kingdom of God like?" Jesus' actions answer that question. The kingdom involves liberation, healing, and release for captives. How sad that the technical illegality of Jesus' action so shocks and blinds the religious leaders that they cannot appreciate the manifestation of God's kingdom through Jesus' sabbath healing.

Grace remains radical; we can never box it in with standards of propriety. But sometimes those of us living with addicts discover that we are setting limits around how we think God can or can't, will or won't, deal with our loved ones. Maybe we first want to witness what looks to us like proper repentance.

We exercise control in a dual sense when we think this way. First, we're trying to control what goes on in our loved ones' hearts. Second, such thinking springs from a desire to control God. If I'm unconsciously limiting God's action, then I'm no freer than the woman in this story.

Obviously addictive behavior can be both physically and spiritually destructive. But most of our loved ones have many fine qualities outside the area of their addiction. My husband does. He is gifted with many positive characteristics: honesty, fidelity, the readiness to forgive, trust in God's mercy and sovereignty, a rich capacity to minister to hurting people, a deep love of scripture. As I list them all, I realize the perversity of focusing on his areas of struggle rather than on his giftedness.

Above all, we need to balance concern over the damage addictive behavior causes with an awareness that we can't know the full mystery of what goes on in our loved ones' hearts to cause that addiction. We can't second-guess what God will or won't do. The bottom line is this: We can never experience God's realm in our hearts if a controlling or judgmental spirit imprisons us.

Thank you, Jesus, for giving us a vision of what God's kingdom is like through your sabbath healing of this woman. Heal us of any judgmentalism, any tendency to set limits around your love. Release us from our spiritual prisons so we can pray with more power and know the grace of your kingdom. Amen.

36

What Does Jesus Mean by Hate?

LUKE 14:25-33

*"Whoever comes to me and does not hate father and
mother, wife and children, brothers and sisters, yes,
and even life itself, cannot be my disciple."*

JESUS HAS JUST compared entering God's kingdom to
a great banquet whose invitees beg off at the last minute,
offering a mix of excuses based on business or personal
concerns that take priority. Now he pushes the envelope
even farther with these challenging words about the radical
demands of discipleship. Many of these verses are similar
in tone to the passage in Matthew 10 where he sends the
Twelve out on mission. "Whoever loves father or mother
more than me is not worthy of me," he tells them there,
"and whoever loves son or daughter more than me is not
worthy of me" (v. 37). Here he actually calls us to hate
our loved ones for his sake—loved ones in this case being
comprised of members of our nuclear family.

Surely the hate Jesus alludes to can't be meant to result
in bitterness or hostility. After all, growth in the Lord gives
birth to spiritual fruit of love, joy, peace, patience, kindness, generosity, faithfulness, gentleness, and self-control

(Gal. 5:22-23) that presumably spill over into all our relationships. As I reflect on this puzzling exchange, one experience keeps coming to mind.

At a recent Al-Anon meeting, folks were discussing Step 1—accepting our powerlessness over alcohol—when I realized yet again, as if for the first time, that I truly am powerless when it comes to influencing my husband's decision to drink. My turn to speak came, and without pausing to consider my words I heard myself blurt out to the group with an intensity that startled me, "There really is nothing I can do to make him stop drinking. There is absolutely nothing at all!" The passion in my voice cut the air like a knife. My words confessed my weakness, but paradoxically, I felt new strength.

Over the next few days, that sense of strength persisted. One evening when my husband clearly was drinking to excess, I remained calm, objective, detached. The next morning the effects of the alcohol were still discernible, but once again I stayed calm. My one thought was this: *I need to pray for him today and ask the Lord to convict him of how dangerous this really is.* So I did.

The detachment I felt after my Al-Anon outburst enabled me to keep clear boundaries between my husband and myself for a while. For the time being at least destructive emotions no longer overwhelmed me. The significance of the experience moved me to ask why this memory comes back to me now in the context of Jesus' disturbing command to "hate" our loved ones.

I certainly don't hate my husband—not even for Jesus' sake. But my sudden awareness of my powerlessness to influence his drinking and the detachment that came with this realization cleared my mind and calmed my spirit so I could center on Jesus in a new way

When Jesus takes first place in our hearts, our response to his call of discipleship takes precedence over even the sacred bonds of family. We say yes to Jesus and then courageously undertake what Jesus calls us to without fear of incurring the displeasure of family and friends.

Prayer

Lord, when you call us to hate family members it sounds very wrong to our human ears. Help us understand and see that as we put you first in our lives and embrace a healthy spiritual detachment in complex relationships, we will be increasingly able to pray with power for our loved ones. Amen.

37

The Elder Brother in Our Hearts

LUKE 15:11-32

"This son of mine was dead and is alive again;
he was lost and is found!"

THE PARABLE OF THE PRODIGAL SON falls in a sequence of teachings that Jesus addresses to Pharisees and teachers of the law who are angry at Jesus for sharing his message with tax collectors and sinners. We have the parable of the lost sheep and the lost coin. Now we read the beloved story of the lost son who comes to his senses and returns home repentant after squandering his inheritance. He hopes to be treated as a hired servant; instead, his father greets him with lavish joy and love.

The father's moving words—"this son of mine was dead and is alive again; he was lost and is found!"—are directed to the servants who will prepare a celebratory banquet. A bit later on, the father will speak almost identical words to the aggrieved elder brother who resents his father's joy over the younger son's return.

How deeply this story must resonate with parents grieving a son or daughter's addiction! Just the other day an old friend related what he and his son have been going through in the wake of the son's arrest for a Driving While Intoxicated (DWI) citation. There's no alienation—just sorrow, concern, and mutual anxiety for the future. How much harder experiences of this type must be when all communication has broken down, and the grieving parent has no idea what is going on in a child's life! Worst of all must be living with the hardness of heart caused by unforgiveness. Consider the elder brother in this parable, and ponder how his resentment eats away at his spirit.

So now I find myself wondering: *How much of the elder brother's attitude resides in each of us?* I've been doing some heavy-duty spiritual work as I pray into these reflections. Has Carl been making a similar effort in pursuit of his own recovery? Because he hasn't shared his inner process with me, I can't know the answer to that question. Yet I have to confess that I've often assumed he has not worked intentionally toward his recovery and have given way to resentment. Even more perversely, sometimes I've taken offense on the Lord's behalf, as though I can read God's mind and pass judgment in God's stead! Surely this is a lot like the elder brother in this story.

Ironically, I used to read this parable in years past with my own behavior in mind, conscious of my failure to take full advantage of the resources God had bestowed on me. How much more could I have done for Jesus had I been able to get over my anxiety after my first husband left me? What if I had dared to move to a new city and explored alternative Christian communities when I started life afresh? Part of me longed to do this, but I was scared. I wanted the reassurance of the familiar—my friends, my job, the little ranch house I had just bought. I was addicted to security.

Now a more hopeful thought strikes me. Both my husband and I are obviously in a new place today. To marry each other took courage. Who knows what gifts God has for us even now if only we could give ourselves in prayerful abandon to helping each other in our respective areas of struggle. If we get past the fears that keep us from new growth, we will discover nothing but joy in the heart of our heavenly Father.

PRAYER

Lord Jesus, thank you for this parable of the prodigal son. If our joy in the father's welcome is tempered by the elder brother's resentment, help us realize that the elder brother also needs understanding and forgiveness. If we harbor resentment over others' behavior, especially that of addicted loved ones, give us the grace to transcend such attitudes and to pray wholeheartedly for their full restoration. Amen.

38

The Comfort of Jesus' Tears

JOHN 11:1-6, 17-44

Jesus began to weep.

WORD COMES TO JESUS that his friend Lazarus, brother of Mary and Martha in the town of Bethany, has fallen ill. Yet instead of hurrying to his side, he stays where he is for two more days. This decision puzzles his disciples, but he reassures them. "This illness does not lead to death," he tells them. "Rather it is for God's glory, so that the Son of God may be glorified through it."

Jesus knows that Lazarus will die before he reaches Bethany. He even knows that upon his arrival, he will raise Lazarus from the dead. When he finally does arrive in Bethany, both Martha and Mary hurry to meet him, convinced that their brother would not have died had Jesus come sooner. Jesus, deeply moved, "began to weep."

Why does he weep? "See how he loved him!" the onlookers say. Commentators have suggested that Jesus weeps over the people's lack of faith. Yet when Martha protests that if Jesus had been with them Lazarus would have lived, and Jesus responds, "I am the resurrection and the life. Those who believe in me, even though they die, will live," Martha does demonstrate her faith. "Yes, Lord," she says, "I believe that you are the Messiah, the Son of God, the one coming into the world." Only when her sister, Mary, falls at his feet, weeping and repeating Martha's words—"Lord, if you had been here, my brother would not have died"—does Jesus break down. I like to believe that his tears spring in part from his compassion and empathy in the presence of Mary's grief. It does not matter that he knows full well what he is about to do or that he knows Lazarus will come out of the tomb. Jesus in John's Gospel embodies foreknowledge and sovereignty, yes; but this doesn't prevent him from feeling with us. Jesus weeps.

And I weep. I have a small crucifix. When I can't sleep at night and can't even pray, overwhelmed by sadness at the tragedy of addiction and all the pain I witness on every side, I hold that crucifix. There in the palm of my hand, I feel the cross, and I feel Jesus' body. The tactile sensation and my emotional sense of being with the Lord become a kind of prayer. Weeping can be prayer. To weep doesn't mean that we lack faith; it means that we are human. Jesus' tears assures us of that if we feel tempted to doubt it.

I have no idea what the future holds for my husband and me, let alone for the many people who suffer around us. I have no idea what the future holds for the world. But whatever lies in store for us, I take heart that Jesus knows. God will bring good out of whatever happens as long as we continue in our love for the Lord.

I take comfort in the realization that Jesus feels with us in each present moment, each present heartache. He empathizes with us and has compassion; he carries our pain in his own heart. As we face obstacles and illnesses, the temptations and weaknesses in our lives and the lives of our addicted loved ones, we remember Jesus' compassion. Knowing that Jesus weeps can bring healing.

PRAYER

Father God, thank you for the tears Jesus shed at the death of Lazarus. Thank you for what this story tells us about your character—that even as you reign over all, you feel with us in our pain. Help us remember your compassion for us when we feel overwhelmed by sin and suffering, within and without. Amen.

39

The Paradox of Peace

LUKE 19:29-44

*"If you, even you, had only recognized on this day
the things that make for peace!"*

JESUS RIDES TOWARD JERUSALEM on a colt as the crowds flock around him, spreading their cloaks on the road and praising God for the miracles they have seen. The Pharisees express their displeasure. "Teacher, order your disciples to stop," they insist. Then, as Jesus approaches Jerusalem, he weeps over the city: "If you, even you, had only recognized on this day the things that make for peace! But now they are hidden from your eyes."

The leaders in Jesus' day had certain assumptions and expectations about the promised Messiah: Who he would be, what he would do—assumptions that blocked their recognizing Jesus as the Promised One. What assumptions or agendas do we hold on to that keep us from recognizing what Jesus requires of us?

Despite Paul's testimony in Philippians 4:11 about learning to be content in all circumstances and despite Al-Anon's assurance that we can learn to be happy whether the alcoholic is still drinking or not, we may feel convinced that full recovery for the ones we love has to be a precondition for peace. Our viewing life through this lens can blind us to other options God may want us to see.

A passage from *Light in My Darkest Night*, a posthumous compilation of journal entries and remembrances about Catherine Marshall's "dark night of the soul" following the death of her granddaughter, intrigued me. In the chapter titled "Husband/Wife Confrontation" her second husband Len LeSourd relates a discussion he and Catherine had over his failed first marriage to an alcoholic. Refusing to buy into Len's excuse that it had been necessary for him to leave his first wife in order to find the creative life God had for him, Catherine poses a provocative question: What if God's perfect plan had been for Len to stick it out with Eve [his first wife], praying for the strength to build a fruitful life of his own right there in the marriage?

I don't mean to imply that I think separation can never be right in marriage to an addicted spouse. Often separation is essential and may provide the catalyst for a loved one's ultimate recovery. In his online testimony, John Baker, a reformed alcoholic and the founder of Saddleback Church's "Celebrate Recovery" program, writes that when he was still drinking heavily, his wife gave him the choice of either seeking help or leaving. Much to her surprise, he chose to leave. During their separation he bottomed out, eventually returning to the marriage and finding his fruitful ministry. Similarly, it was after several years' separation that Joy McClain's husband finally found sobriety, and their marriage was restored. She tells her story in *Waiting for His Heart: Lessons from a Wife Who Chose to Stay.*

What could happen if each of us looked beyond our preconceived assumptions about what we think we need and asked Jesus for his perspective on what would bring us peace? What would happen if we listened for his answer—searching our hearts, seeking the guidance of counselors or friends, and immersing ourselves in scripture?

Prayer

Gracious God, scripture tells us that your thoughts are not our thoughts nor your ways our ways. When we are trapped in dead-end thinking over struggles with addicted loved ones, help us call this to mind. In honesty and vulnerability, may we ask you what will bring us peace. Give us the grace to seek your answer and follow the path you show us—one step at a time. Amen.

40

The Challenge of a Biblical Anger

MARK 11:15-18

[Jesus] entered the temple and began to drive out those who were selling.

THIS ACCOUNT OF JESUS' righteous anger at the Temple money changers is charged with power. I'll never forget when I stumbled on John's version of this story in a motel room by the sea. My husband and I had planned a restorative mini-retreat for the night, but things went south after he chose to drink.

Jesus' anger in this story is clearly intentional; he has not fallen into a mindless temper tantrum that overrides his will and makes him a slave to his emotions. My anger that night differed greatly from the anger of Jesus. My anger, a helpless mix of frustration and despair, erupted from my heart in a manner that was quite out of my control. Yet, as I've been praying into these Gospel passages, the Holy Spirit has begun to teach me important lessons.

Obviously, indulging angry feelings and letting them spill out uncontrollably is useless. While undisciplined venting is seldom good, recognizing and accepting our anger at the damage addiction causes is both necessary and healthy. Ephesians 4:26 tells us to be angry but not to sin. So the question becomes, What can we do with our anger? How can we put its energy to constructive use? If we ask Jesus to help us with this, surely he will answer that prayer.

We can use anger constructively by reflecting on the feelings it may be camouflaging, feelings we need to understand if we're to deal with the situation more fruitfully. I've begun to realize how my anger often masks my grief and sadness over the tragedy of addiction. By getting in touch with these feelings, I pray more deeply—just as remaining trapped in a spirit of resentment inhibits prayer. Then too, the more I've explored my inner psyche, the more I've realized that subconsciously I direct much of my anger at myself. It springs from despair over my own helplessness to control my feelings as well as from frustration at my husband's choices. Insights like this can be great resources for growth.

Finally, I think it's critical to remind ourselves of our loved ones' unique strengths and gifts. This remembrance creates balance and integration—much like stepping back from a picture so we can absorb its details in proper perspective. Along these lines, I've found it helpful to pray into Philippians 4:8 and to call that verse to mind when I'm having trouble dealing with my anger. It can be powerful to apply Paul's advice to think about "whatever is true, whatever is honorable, whatever is just, whatever is pure, whatever is pleasing, whatever is commendable" when we're thinking about addicted loved ones.

Yes, in contrast to our outbursts of temper, Jesus' rage at the Temple money changers was rooted in zealous and holy righteousness. Rather than being discouraged about our misguided or misdirected anger, we can ask him to help us deal more fruitfully with our anger. At the same time, we remind ourselves to direct our anger at the demon of addiction and the damage that it causes—not at our addicted loved ones.

Prayer

God of peace, we often fall prey to sinful expressions of anger when we feel at the end of our rope over a loved one's addiction. May we be angry but not sin. Restore our sense of balance so that we remember our loved ones' good qualities and gifts when our equilibrium is threatened. When the time is right, teach us how to speak the truth in love. In the name of Jesus we pray. Amen.

41

Codependency vs. Surrender to the Lord

JOHN 12:20-26

"Unless a grain of wheat falls into the earth and dies, it remains just a single grain; but if it dies, it bears much fruit."

PEOPLE'S FASCINATION WITH JESUS is mounting. He has entered Jerusalem in triumph, riding on a donkey, acclaimed by the crowds after miraculously raising Lazarus from the tomb. Everyone wants to see him, but the clamor of curiosity prompts him to remind his listeners that a lot more is at stake here than the excitement of a miraculous sign. "The hour has come for the Son of Man to be glorified," he announces. Read: "killed." "Very truly, I tell you, unless a grain of wheat falls into the earth and dies, it remains just a single grain; but if it dies, it bears much fruit."

Following Jesus takes on new implications here. Earlier in his ministry, people followed simply by accompanying him on his preaching and healing journeys, listening and watching, marveling at his words and his miracles. But now, to follow Jesus means accompanying him to the cross. He reminds the crowd that the one who loves his or her life will lose it, while the one who hates his or her life in this world will keep it eternally. This "otherworldly" promise seems hard to grasp when we're feeling vulnerable and scared. Perhaps this explains why Jesus couches it in the language of poetry, clothes it in beautiful down-to-earth imagery: "Unless a grain of wheat falls into the earth and dies, it remains just a single grain; but if it dies, it bears much fruit."

This lovely imagery encourages some of us, when we're at our most idealistic and superspiritual, to imagine ourselves dying to self and becoming the seed that falls to the ground for the sake of others in ways Jesus never intended. Certain moods can all too easily draw us into this sort of thinking, fancying ourselves giving and giving in saintly ways that in wiser moments we would recognize as unhealthy codependency. At times I have fallen prey to misguided visions, dreaming of ways I might become the cure for my husband's alcoholism if I could just learn to love him in better ways. Even now I'm occasionally tempted in this direction, but now I catch myself and rein in the fantasies.

I recognize this tendency in others. I think of a woman I know who was recently mourning the end of a love relationship with an alcoholic partner (they were not married). The more we talked, the clearer it seemed that this relationship had been terribly destructive for them both and that it was a great mercy it was now over. However, she felt that Jesus had been calling her to die to self in this relationship—to go to the cross, as it were, in the context of their love—and now that her partner had left, life had lost its meaning. Her deep grief kept me from "preaching," but I did ask her ever so gently if Jesus might actually be calling her to die to self in a way that differed from what she imagined. What if he was calling her to release some of the hopes and dreams she had invested in that relationship in order to free her to move into deeper relationship with the Lord and new growth in him?

Now I find myself asking, What in me needs to fall to the ground and die so I can give birth to greater fruitfulness? What needs to die in us if we are to come into full and faithful creativity—for Jesus, for others, and for ourselves? How does Jesus want to prune us and discipline us so we can love him more? Can we learn to love ourselves *and* the addicts in our lives in spiritually healthier ways?

PRAYER

Jesus, we confess that when you talk about dying to self for the sake of your call, we have mixed responses. At times we may want to turn away; at other times we hear your words and receive them eagerly, though sometimes we embrace them in a codependent spirit. Give us wisdom to hear your words in the right way and courage to respond to them as you would have us to. Amen.

42

Marriage and the Kingdom of Heaven

MATTHEW 22:23-33

"In the resurrection they neither marry nor are given in marriage."

THE SADDUCEES, WHO DIDN'T BELIEVE in the resurrection, test Jesus by posing a hypothetical scenario. Say that a woman who has been sequentially married to seven brothers, each of whom died and left her childless, finally dies as well. Whose wife will she be in the resurrection? Jesus replies with the verse above. Then he zeroes in on the real issue, namely the resurrection itself.

Many years ago, when my first husband was ending our marriage, Jesus' love broke over me in extraordinary ways. One day after collapsing in tears at the prospect of our impending divorce, in my mind's ear I heard these words: "'In the resurrection they neither marry nor are given in marriage.'" Peace flooded my heart.

I wasn't sure what had happened, but as time went on and I began to build a new life as a single-again woman, insights started to crystallize. I might not have a marriage any longer here on earth, but marriage, this verse told me, is not the be all and end all. An experience far richer and more glorious awaited me in the kingdom of heaven.

Today I am married again; but that lesson and the eternal perspective it set forth remains with me. If we approach marriage expecting it to solve all our problems and save us, we will find our hopes dashed. Carl and I had the passage in Ephesians 5 (on the reciprocal roles of husband and wife) read at our wedding. But what man, especially an addicted man, loves his wife sacrificially as Christ loves the church? And what wife with struggles of her own can always submit to her husband? No, hoping for an "ideal" marriage is surely a setup for disaster.

But what if we see marriage as a training ground for living more fully now and then on into the future of God's kingdom? We practice loving as we are called to love. We practice praying. We try to see our spouses objectively and honestly, getting past all the emotional turbulence that addiction can cause and asking God what lessons we are meant to absorb. We can, and should, also look beyond marriage itself and practice being in community with others, widening our spiritual and relational horizons. We can work at growing into more fruitful and faithful members of Christ's body on earth.

And, yes, to return to marriage, we may find we can increasingly practice agape love with our spouses when we feel hurt and let down. We can open ourselves and our hearts to let God work in us.

Finally, when we feel disillusioned and discouraged and perhaps long for a more ideal marriage than the one in which we find ourselves, we can discover renewal by praying over the provocative promise Jesus offers here, that "in the resurrection they neither marry nor are given in marriage." We can ask the Lord for a change of heart that helps us embrace an eternal perspective. With the Holy Spirit's help we may live into the kingdom here and now as we open ourselves to new growth with the loved ones in our lives.

PRAYER

Master Teacher, those of us in marriages troubled by addiction deal with particular struggles. Help us see marriage not just as a relationship to bring us personal fulfillment but as a gracious training ground—your training ground—for learning to love in agape ways that will stretch our hearts and fashion us into the people you want us to be. Give us a kingdom-of-heaven vision, an eternal perspective that will transcend shortsighted expectations and desires. Amen.

43

Readiness, Responsibility, and Recognition

MATTHEW 24:3-13

"The one who endures to the end will be saved."

On Wednesday of Holy Week Jesus' disciples come to him in private to ask him about "the end of the age." He steeps his reply in apocalyptic imagery. He talks about "wars and rumors of wars," about escalating conflicts and natural disasters that will be "the beginning of the birth pangs." There will be persecutions, he warns, and increasing wickedness. Still, "the one who endures to the end will be saved."

The discourse intensifies. We have the parable of ten virgins (bridesmaids) awaiting the bridegroom, five of whom have trimmed their lamps to be ready at a moment's notice and five unprepared ones who are caught off guard. We have the parable of the talents, which contrasts two wise servants who have responsibly invested their master's money with the cowardly one who has hidden his talent in the ground. Finally, we read the stark parable in which the king separates the nations into two groups, as one would separate sheep from goats, and commends those who cared for him on finding him hungry, thirsty, a stranger, naked, and imprisoned, but condemns those who did not. In response to the bewilderment of his listeners who don't know when this happened, the king of the parable tells them, "Just as you did it to one of the least of these who are members of my family, you did it to me" (Matt. 25:40).

While these judgment parables seem frightening, taken together they illustrate how we are to endure to the end in our own lives. But what exactly are they asking us to do? As I read this passage over, three *R*s seem highlighted for me: *readiness*, *responsibility*, and *recognition*. The wise virgins have taken care to be ready for the arrival of the bridegroom at any moment. The wise servants have behaved responsibly with their master's money. And those whom the king (Jesus) commends for having cared for him on finding him hungry, thirsty, a stranger, naked, and imprisoned, have recognized the human dignity of their suffering brothers and sisters, even if they didn't recognize Jesus himself in their need.

Though on the surface Jesus commends behavior, the attitudes of the heart are essential here. Jesus praises the people who have understood what matters. They have kept their spirits attuned to the right priorities. The ecumenical Church of the Saviour structures itself around concepts of "the journey inward" and "the journey outward." Members there commit to a daily discipline of prayer and reflection and to service at some point of the world's need. These spiritual disciplines are not viewed as works but rather as means to cultivate receptive attitudes of readiness, responsibility, and recognition. Then Jesus, through the Holy Spirit, can work in people's hearts and lead them along paths of discipleship uniquely suited to them.

The tragedy of addiction with its soul-numbing effects blocks those in its clutches from consistently living in this fashion. All of us have stunted responses, personal addictions from which we need to recover. All serious Christians must guard against the temptation to buy into the values of our culture. Spending time with other believers will help us remain faithful and, by implication, "endure to the end."

Prayer

Lord God, help us "endure to the end" by cultivating the right priorities in our lives. Help us transcend codependency and other addictions so that we can grow in the love and service to which you call us. We pray this in Jesus' name. Amen.

44

Obeying God's Nudges in Our Hearts

MARK 14:12-16

"[The man] will show you a large room upstairs, furnished and ready."

ON THE THURSDAY NIGHT before his death, Jesus tells his disciples to go into the city where a man with a water jar will meet them, waiting to lead them to a specific house. There the owner of the house will show them a large upper room, furnished and ready, where the disciples are to prepare for the Passover meal that Jesus will celebrate with them. They go into the city and find everything exactly as Jesus told them they would.

I wonder about the owner of that house. *Who is he?* Clearly someone has told him that the room will be needed for that Passover celebration. How much more does he know? Does he know the significance of what will take place there? Is he aware of the contribution he makes by readying that room? And how does this story apply to us?

When we sense a request from Jesus of us, even if we don't understand the reason, are we as ready to listen and faithfully follow instructions? How often are we aware of the Lord's placing such a request on our hearts?

I remember one evening, after my husband had been drinking and had gone to bed, when I felt the strong impression that I should go into the bedroom and lie down beside him. I didn't want to do this; I simply wanted to get away, perhaps go and spend some time with a friend. Still, I obeyed that nudge (from God?). A spirit of loving detachment came over me, and a significant conversation unfolded between Carl and myself. I spoke words that ordinarily I couldn't have spoken. But I sensed God wanted me to share them with him that night.

Did my husband remember this conversation the next morning? I have no idea, for we never mentioned it again. Still, to obey that nudge felt important, and my own experience of speaking those words lovingly, calmly, and firmly encouraged me. I could acknowledge that I had grown more than I might have realized at a time when I desperately needed a boost in morale.

If the detachment to which God calls us with addicted loved ones often takes the form of wise and healthy withdrawal from a fruitless conversation, God desired something more from me here. In this case God wanted me to step back from my own emotionality. I believe God wanted me to steady myself—to let myself be steadied—to the point that I could quietly and calmly make myself available in that moment to my husband. I'm thankful that I could respond positively.

Ever-present God, we pray that you will show us those steps you want us to take, those actions you want us to perform that will yield fruit in our own and others' lives. Make us alert to messages you send us through the advice or requests of friends, through particular verses of scripture, through listening prayer. Give us a genuine desire to hear from you and to follow in the direction that you lead. Amen.

45

Resources for Radical Love

JOHN 13:33-38; 15:1-11

*"Just as I have loved you, you also
should love one another."*

*"Just as the branch cannot bear
fruit by itself unless it abides in the vine,
neither can you unless you abide in me".*

WE ARE IN THE UPPER ROOM on the evening of
Maundy Thursday. Judas has just left to arrange his betrayal
of Jesus. Speaking to the remaining eleven, Jesus explains
he will be with them only a little longer and that where he
is going they cannot come. Then he says, "I give you a new
commandment, that you love one another. Just as I have
loved you, you also should love one another."

This command is indeed new, for it is neither the
generic love of neighbor at one end of the spectrum nor
the intimate love of family and spouse at the other. Jesus
calls for a sacrificial commitment to the body of Christ, a
kingdom-of-heaven vision that takes us out of ourselves
in a new way, transforming us totally if we can embrace
it. This command has intimate ties to his impending crucifixion and to the situation in which his followers will

find themselves after he is gone. The disciples, of course, are completely out of touch with what is at stake. Peter, the impulsive, self-confident optimist, embodies it all by declaring, "I will lay down my life for you." Jesus sounds the sober note of reality in his response, "Before the cock crows, you will have denied me three times," but the grim truth of that prophecy goes right over Peter's head. In John's Gospel we don't hear Peter's response; but in Matthew and Mark, Peter declares that even if he has to die with Jesus, he will never disown him—and the other disciples say the same.

What about us? Can we obey this new commandment? Certainly we can't do so alone. But then, that's the whole point; that's what makes the verse in John 15:4 so essential. What is at stake here has little to do with us as individuals and everything to do with our sacrificial belonging to Jesus and his body. After he and the disciples have left the upper room following the Last Supper and set out for the garden of Gethsemane, Jesus tells them, "Just as the branch cannot bear fruit by itself unless it abides in the vine, neither can you unless you abide in me." His words are inextricably interwoven with his earlier command that we love one another in the cross-bearing way that he loves each of us, which transcends personal need.

Those of us with addicted loved ones may feel especially unequal to this challenge, as the pain and chaos of living with addiction can often deplete us. Yet we need the support of this interconnected body.

Despite language about withering branches being thrown to the fire, I can't believe Jesus means that when we fail to abide and obey, God will no longer love us. Nor can he mean that when we *do* abide we are chalking up moral merit. God's love remains steady. When we disobey, it is we who choose temporarily to step out of that close relationship. Then we cause pain—to God, to ourselves, and to one another. "I have said these things to you," Jesus tells his disciples, "so that my joy may be in you, and that your joy may be complete." The natural imagery Jesus uses here, of the branch abiding in the vine, makes it clear that our capacity to love doesn't spring from our own effort but is the fruit of the Holy Spirit—the Counselor, the Spirit of Truth—whom Jesus promises to send.

Prayer

Lord Jesus, we thank you for your moving farewell discourse to the disciples before your crucifixion, your prayers for them and all who have believed in you through the ages. Help us meditate on your call to relinquish a narrow individuality in favor of a deep belonging to your entire body of believers. If struggles with our own addictions and those of our loved ones hold us back, encourage and guide us. May we see our need for this deeper fellowship; help us create it for others. Amen.

46

The Temptation Not to Pray

MARK 14:32-38

"Keep awake and pray that you may not come into the time of trial."

JESUS TAKES PETER, JAMES, AND JOHN with him as he prays in Gethsemane the night before the crucifixion. "Remain here, and keep awake," he tells them. Falling to the ground a short distance away, he prays for deliverance from what is about to befall him and then returns to find them sleeping. "Simon, are you asleep?" he asks. "Keep awake and pray that you may not come into the time of trial; the spirit indeed is willing, but the flesh is weak."

Sometimes when others (or perhaps we ourselves) fall down on the job and drop some assigned task, our reflexive response is, "Remember, you're only human. Don't be too hard on yourself." I doubt that any of us would have reassured those sleeping disciples in such an enabling way. At the same time, can we honestly say we would have done better in their place? Certainly I can't.

"Pray so that you will not fall into temptation" (NIV). Often I have wanted to say these words to my husband. Even as I write this, I realize that instead of exhorting my husband, what I need to do is pray more faithfully myself. Just like Jesus' disciples, despite all God has been teaching me about prayer, sometimes I succumb to the temptation not to pray!

In an earlier meditation I wondered if many of our struggles in prayer stem from an inability to let go of cherished scenarios about when and how we want our prayers answered. What might happen if we could relinquish those completely and abandon ourselves with open-ended faith into God's sovereign care? Now, reading about those sleeping disciples, I find myself raising this question again. It strikes me that while attachment to personal agendas does underlie many of our struggles in prayer, in this passage the problem is much larger. "I am deeply grieved, even to death," Jesus tells Peter, James, and John before leaving them to pray in the garden of Gethsemane and begging them to be with him in spirit. Jesus, their Lord, the One on whose teachings, miracles, and power they have always depended now asks for their help in a time of personal crisis. Is the weight of this request too much for the disciples to handle? Do their spirits shut down?

We often feel overwhelmed by crises, but our challenges aren't as steep as the one Jesus' disciples face. We aren't watching as our Lord confesses vulnerability and asks for our support. But our personal encounters both with the tragedy of addiction and with our own dysfunctional responses can seem overwhelming. Perhaps our spirits do shut down, even though we realize we are being called to pray. Maybe we can't summon the strength to face the challenge.

At times when we feel overwhelmed by the enormity of prayer needs, it's important for us to remember the rest of the story—how Jesus rose from the grave after his agony in the garden of Gethsemane and his crucifixion and then how he encouraged his followers before he ascended. We remember his promise to send the Helper, the Holy Spirit, to comfort us and intercede for us. This comfort and intercession buoy us up past our despair when the call to prayer overwhelms our spirits.

Prayer

Father God, we thank you for the promise that the Holy Spirit intercedes for us in ways we cannot understand. When we feel overwhelmed with the crises we face and the suffering we see, fill our hearts with your encouragement, compassion, and wisdom. Restored in our own spirits we can then pray with power. Amen.

47

Daring to Draw Closer to the Cross

Luke 22:47-54
But Peter was following at a distance.

As Jesus returns to the sleeping disciples after his anguished prayer in the garden, Judas arrives with an armed crowd and greets him with a kiss; Jesus is betrayed, arrested, and abandoned. At the house of the high priest Anna questions him and then sends him, still bound, to the high priest Caiaphas for further questioning. All three synoptic Gospels tell us that Peter follows at a distance. Perhaps in his mind he hears and agonizes over Jesus' earlier words: "If any want to become my followers, let them deny themselves and take up their cross and follow me" (Matt. 16:24).

What would it mean to take up our personal crosses and follow Jesus? When we're bowed down with suffering posed by a loved one's addiction, we may be unable to contemplate any more pain or hardship. Bearing hypothetical future crosses can feel too staggering to imagine. The stresses and sorrows of our present circumstances can feel like a heavier burden than we can carry. How then can we tolerate the thought that Jesus may have even weightier challenges for us in the years to come?

Of course, closeness to Jesus always involves a deeper encounter with reality and an acknowledgment that the future will hold new challenges. But Jesus doesn't want us to dwell on hypothetical horrors that haven't even happened. When the emerging moment gives us crosses to bear—those that inevitably come with living and loving—he never leaves us to shoulder those burdens alone. If we cry out to Jesus in our exhaustion and pain, challenges become opportunities to grow into deeper intimacy with the Lord.

Do we still fear? Do we follow at a distance? What if coming closer to Jesus also means facing up to the darker sides of our nature that we prefer to ignore? We may not want to get in touch emotionally with God's perspective on certain areas of sin in our lives. What might Jesus ask us to give up? Will we be called to relinquish idols to which we have been addicted? What about habits or agendas we desperately want to protect? Surely our addicted loved ones experience these fears when they consider committing to recovery. But don't we face them as well?

In his book *The Great Divorce*, C. S. Lewis records a fantasy about a busload of ghosts who take a day trip to visit heaven. He writes of the encounter between a certain ghost and the angel who comes to meet him. The angel asks the ghost to let him kill his most precious sin, personified as a small lizard who sits on his shoulder, whispering temptations into his ear. Terrified, the ghost agrees. He is convinced he will die, but amazingly, as the angel breaks the lizard's neck and throws it to the ground, both ghost and lizard begin to grow brighter and more solid. The ghost becomes a strong young man, the lizard a magnificent stallion. As the man mounts the stallion and they ride off toward the mountains, the landscape reverberates with song.[*]

As I write this, tears stream down my cheeks. I find myself spontaneously praying for my husband's change of heart so he might truly desire and find sobriety. At the same time, I consider my own sin—the ongoing burden of anger, faithlessness, discouragement, and fear—and pray that I too will experience a change of heart.

PRAYER

Lord Jesus, transform us so we no longer follow at a distance. Empower us to accompany you to the cross and lay our lives at your feet. Give us the courage to offer you any sins and temptations we clutch in our hands and bury in our hearts. Redeem us, heal us, and bring us to new life in you. Amen.

[*] *The Great Divorce*, C. S. Lewis (New York: Collier Books/Macmillan, 1946), 98–105.

48

The Agony of Abandonment

MARK 15:33-34

"My God, my God, why have you forsaken me?"

JESUS HANGS ON THE CROSS. At the sixth hour darkness covers the land until the ninth hour, and at the ninth hour he utters this scream of agony and abandonment. Yes, he experiences terrible physical pain, but the spiritual pain is surely worse. Sometimes in our own lives we can be pierced by an almost mythic awareness of the sin that grips this fallen world, perhaps through a seemingly minor incident. I remember driving along the highway when out of the corner of my eye I spotted the mangled bloody body of a bird by the side of the road and instantly burst into tears. For one brief second I glimpsed how carelessly we can destroy vulnerability and innocence.

If we humans can feel such grief over a small and fleeting thing, how can we begin to imagine Jesus' spiritual agony as he carried the weight of the world's sin on his shoulders? Couple this with his apparent sense of abandonment by God. Theological explanations aside, Jesus seems nakedly human here, completely stripped of omniscience and foreknowledge.

Alyssa Phillips   157

The first time I read Psalm 22 and realized that Jesus' cry is actually the first line of that psalm, I felt a little better. As the psalm progresses, it shifts back and forth between agony in the present moment and remembrance of God's past faithfulness, bringing the psalmist at last to a place of restored faith. The words of this psalm must have run through Jesus' mind as he hung there on the cross; perhaps its message brought comfort. At least, that was my hope. Still, that scream of agony couldn't be completely softened.

Some people's lives, including a few I know who have struggled with loved ones' addictions, seem so fraught with suffering that in order to survive spiritually, I imagine they go back and forth in their minds between the pain of the present and their memories of God's faithfulness. I think of a friend who has been in ministry for years with addicts and the homeless, facing along the way so many ongoing crises with loved ones in her own life that I stand in awe of her deep faith. Do people in her situation develop endurance in times of pain by dipping into the well of memory, strengthening themselves as they recall the ways God has supported them in the past?

When my husband and I go through tough times, I think back on past blessings to fortify myself. But I'm well aware that my own pain is miniscule compared with the pain of others and the pain Jesus endured.

I recently reflected that when I can't sleep and feel overwhelmed with sadness or fear, I cling to a crucifix as though I'm physically clinging to Jesus. That my own difficulties can't begin to compare with the suffering of so many others, let alone with Jesus' suffering, somehow ceases to matter at these times. The global pain merges with the pain in my heart, eliminating self-consciousness; as I hold that crucifix in the palm of my hand, I feel I'm with Jesus at the cross. I remember how he cried out in his own agony, bewilderment, and forsakenness. I realize that his cry covers us all, covers everything any of us have suffered or can suffer. Mysteriously that cry brings healing.

PRAYER

Lord, your suffering on the cross seems too staggering for words. Forgive us for the times our obsession with personal problems imprisons us in solitary pain and we forget the suffering of others and yours on the cross. Forgive us, Lord, for the ways we have failed you and continue to fail you. Have mercy on us in our weakness, and may we bear in mind that you absorb our sin and redeem us through your death on the cross. Amen.

49

Jesus' Victory and Our Ultimate Hope

JOHN 19:25-30
"It is finished."

HERE IS JESUS' VICTORY CRY. In John's Gospel, Jesus seems to transcend much of his human vulnerability throughout the crucifixion, to be in more spiritual control than we witness in the synoptic Gospels. "Woman, here is your son," he tells his mother. To John he says, "Here is your mother." A bit later, in order to fulfill scripture, he says, "I am thirsty" and receives the sponge soaked in wine vinegar. Finally he utters the triumphant cry, "It is finished." How vastly this account in John differs from Mark's stark recollection of our Lord's last agonizing scream.

I take minimal comfort in Mark's account from knowing that Jesus' cry of agony quotes Psalm 22 and that the progression back and forth between agony and faith in that psalm ultimately culminates in faith. Here in John, as evidenced by the triumphant words "It is finished," the comfort seems greater; Jesus fully understands the necessity of his pain and why he has been given this cross to endure. I like to believe that as he hung there on Good Friday, the words of Isaiah 53:4—"Surely he has borne our infirmities and carried our diseases"—were going through his mind. Whether we think of the cross mainly as the instrument of our personal salvation or primarily as Jesus' victory over the world's sin, the grand cosmic job has finally been accomplished, and Jesus knows it.

Can we uncover meaning in our strivings by trusting in an eternal perspective we do not fully understand? Can we believe that God will ultimately transform and redeem the chaos and pain of watching our loved ones in the grip of addictions?

We have all failed in many ways. The addicts we love have failed, and we have failed time and again, despite our resolutions—all our promises to ourselves, to God, and to our loved ones. But Jesus did not and does not fail. In a January 2012 sermon titled "Marriage in Christ," Rev. Tim Keller speaks of Jesus as the ultimate and perfect spouse to each one of us. Jesus emptied himself and came to earth to give himself for us, even dying on the cross for our redemption and remaining there as we, such poor spouses to him, reviled and mocked him. When the Holy Spirit enables us to experience Jesus' spousal love in our hearts, says Keller, then we will receive the power to love more faithfully.

We may sometimes despair of seeing our loved ones freed from addiction; we may despair of rising above our own addictions to anger, depression, guilt, or fear. But just as Jesus cried, "It is finished" from the cross, we can affirm that ultimately our own struggles and sorrows will be redemptively healed in God's kingdom—whether or not we experience full healing here on earth.

When our trust falters, we can ask the Lord to restore it through the power of the Holy Spirit. As we struggle in relationships with the addicts in our lives, the gift of an enduring trust becomes our most precious resource.

PRAYER

Father God, we thank you that Jesus triumphed over his suffering to rejoice in the completion of his redemptive task. He saw with the eyes of his spirit the renewal of all and the conquering of the world's evil through his sacrificial death. Give us this eternal perspective in our endeavors with addicted loved ones. Help us know that because of his sacrificial death and triumphant resurrection, the day will come when we too will see clearly that all is being made new. Amen.

50

Glimpses of a Larger Reality

LUKE 24:13-35

Then [the disciples'] eyes were opened, and they recognized him; and he vanished from their sight.

JESUS HAS RISEN! "Two of them"—we don't know who—encounter the risen Jesus on the road to Emmaus but are "kept from recognizing him." When he asks them what they have been discussing on their walk, they pour out bewilderment and sorrow: Jesus, who was going to redeem Israel, was instead crucified, dashing their hopes. They explain how some women told them about finding the empty tomb and seeing a vision of angels announcing that Jesus was risen. Clearly, these two don't believe the women. Jesus rebukes them for their lack of faith, and beginning with Moses and the prophets, proceeds to explain scriptural prophecies about himself. When they urge him to stay with them at their village and have supper, he does; as he breaks the bread and gives it to them, "their eyes were opened, and they recognized him; and he vanished from their sight." Hurrying to Jerusalem, the two testify to the eleven of their experience and of their recognizing Jesus "in the breaking of the bread."

Alyssa Phillips 163

This story has always moved me, especially in this one detail: Their eyes fail to recognize Jesus until the breaking of the bread. Mary also fails to recognize him when she sees him at the empty tomb and takes him to be the gardener. Only when he calls her by name does she cry out, "Rabbouni!" (John 20:16).

There's something supernatural about this failure to recognize Jesus. Significantly, once realization dawns, we read that "their eyes were opened"—not "they opened their eyes." But there's also something familiar about failing to recognize an infinitely precious person whom we feared we had lost but who unexpectedly joins us again. I remember years ago bumping into a beloved friend I had not seen for a decade and being totally bewildered as I gazed at him. Obviously puzzled by my lack of response, he came over to me, took my hand, and said, "Why, it's me—Jimmy!"

To recognize the risen Jesus is to acknowledge more than our Lord's unique resurrection; it is to become aware of a whole new reality. The impossible is possible and has actually come to pass.

Occasionally we briefly glimpse a larger reality in just this way. One morning I woke up after a bad incident the previous evening and looked at my husband lying asleep beside me. As I studied the vulnerability on his face, all my anguish from the night before dissolved into a tender awareness of how "other" he is. Everything I hear in Al-Anon about alcoholism being "cunning and baffling" struck me as profoundly true. We are all such mysteries; surely each of us is truly known only by God.

And then in a flash, all my husband's good qualities came flooding over me: his fidelity and honesty, his readiness to forgive and forget my own turbulent outbursts, his faith despite the temptations that beset him.

What must it have cost him to have absorbed so often the flood of my own frustration? Yet that frustration came from my heart. How complex we all are! What a miracle it is that so many of us manage not only to live with each other but, by God's grace, to grow in love and understanding over the years! Tears came to my eyes, and I felt a passionate gratitude for the gift—yes, the gift—of being married to this man.

Prayer

Thank you, Lord, for the times in our lives when we get a brief glimpse of a larger reality that is often hidden from us. While we know that these experiences can't compare with the glimpses of you that the disciples and Mary experienced after your resurrection, we give you thanks for them. Help us remember the insights we gained at these times so we can continue to see the world and especially our addicted loved ones through eyes that have been touched by your Spirit. Amen.

51

Believing What We Have Not Yet Seen

JOHN 20:19-29

"Blessed are those who have not seen and yet have come to believe."

IT IS THE FIRST DAY of the week, right after Mary Magdalene's encounter with the risen Lord. Now Jesus suddenly appears among the disciples in the room where they have been hiding. He blesses them, shows them his hands and his side. Thomas is not present; later, when the others tell him what has happened, he refuses to believe. A week later the disciples are again in the same house, and this time Thomas is there. Once more Jesus comes through the locked door; once more he says, "Peace be with you." Now he addresses Thomas personally, "Put your finger here and see my hands. Reach out your hand and put it in my side. Do not doubt but believe." Thomas then utters his famous testimony: "My Lord and my God!"

Doubting Thomas has an unfair reputation. In Luke's account *all* the disciples are "startled and frightened" when Jesus appears for the first time, thinking they are seeing a ghost. Even after he reassures them they remain "disbelieving and still wondering" till he eats a piece of broiled fish in their presence. (See Luke 24:37-43.)

"Blessed are those who have not seen and yet have come to believe." Jesus speaks these words to Thomas, foreshadowing our own challenge, since today we cannot see the spiritual body of the risen Jesus in the same way those first disciples saw him. And yet. . . . And yet. . . .

When my mother was dying of cancer, my father provided care for her at home. Both were in their late eighties. Each weekend I drove to New Jersey to be with them, but one night I had to jump in the car midweek to make the trip. Daddy had been drinking too much during this stressful time and had landed in the emergency room after a bad fall. He stayed in the hospital for several days, being treated for his injury and detoxifying from the alcohol. One night, in a kind of delirium, he thought the nurse entering his room was a ghost, and he cried out in fear. "Touch me," she told him. "Look, a ghost doesn't have flesh and bones the way I do." Daddy touched her outstretched hand and found courage. Days later, after returning home, he never took another drink, caring for Mother faithfully until she died a few months later.

My father was still an agnostic at that time. Five years later, in his mid-nineties, a friend of mine led him to Jesus shortly before his own death. But often I have wondered, *Hadn't Jesus already touched him that night, mediated through the wisdom of that inspired nurse?*

Thinking back to daddy's hospital experience and his subsequent sobriety, I've sometimes wondered wistfully if Carl would choose permanent sobriety in order to care for me were I ever to need him. These days I've ceased to speculate about this—partly because Carl has begun to change in important ways recently and partly because the Lord has been working in my own heart through these scriptural reflections. I've stopped worrying about the future; I am actually beginning to live one day at a time.

The message of the Resurrection affirms that whatever we endure in our fallen world, it won't be the final reality. The real issue is not what Carl will or won't do; it is whether I can trust Jesus to be there when my time of need comes. Journeying in prayer through the Gospels, has deepened my trust that this will indeed be so. May all of us who struggle with the challenge of living with addicted loved ones receive the gift of such trust.

Prayer

Father God, we thank you for the gift of the Resurrection narratives in the pages of the Gospels. Thank you for continuing to reveal yourself to us today. May our experiences of your presence transform us. As we hold them in our hearts, we will know you are indeed the One on whom we can always depend. Amen.

52

The Promise of Jesus' Eternal Presence

MATTHEW 28:16-20

*"And remember, I am with you always,
to the end of the age."*

SHORTLY BEFORE HIS ASCENSION Jesus calls the eleven to a mountain, where he tells them that full authority has been granted to him in heaven and on earth. At the same time he gives them "the Great Commission," telling them to go into every nation, baptizing believers and teaching them to obey all the commandments. "And remember," he concludes, "I am with you always, to the end of the age."

This kind of evangelism presupposes our deep growth in the Lord and in fellowship with other believers; we can't undertake such tasks by ourselves. Those of us with addicted loved ones may have trouble imagining ourselves living such a fruitful Christian life. When we feel discouraged, we recall Jesus' assurance that all things are possible for God and take heart in knowing that his promise to be with us "to the end of the age" is unconditional. It doesn't depend on our accomplishing those high spiritual goals.

In fact, as I consider the challenges I've described in these pages, Jesus' promise to be with us to the end of the age offers the most comforting message we could receive. I have experienced his constant presence—loving, challenging, forgiving, healing—in my efforts to live as he calls me and in my relapses along the way. This presence is ours as we reach out to him in our own journeys.

A central premise underlying everything I've written here is that, just as Al-Anon counsels, the best way to live with addicted loved ones comes in embracing the call to seek our own spiritual growth rather than dwelling on their behavior. Paradoxically, the best influence we can have will probably come as we step out of the way and give those we love the space to encounter God themselves. Most important, perhaps, is that we can pray—especially as we steep ourselves in scripture.

How could I have anticipated when I shut myself up in a motel bathroom at a time of despair over my husband's drinking that my encounter with Jesus' anger toward the Temple money changers would lead me on this journey of scriptural reflection? The journey is far from over, but it has made a tremendous difference in my life. As Jesus has calmed my anger, he has opened my heart to love my husband more deeply, to appreciate and give thanks for the way his gifts continue to bear fruit even as he continues to struggle. He has been changing in so many heartening ways since I've been praying with these Gospel passages. How much of the change I see in him represents objective new growth on his part, and how much reflects my fresh readiness to appreciate qualities that have always been there? My guess is there's a little bit of both. One thing is sure: The Holy Spirit has been working with the two of us, blessing us along this journey. As I wrote in the preface, our life together today differs greatly from our life during the time I worked with these meditations.

I pray that many readers with addicted loved ones will embark on a similar journey, finding with the Holy Spirit's help those scripture verses that speak to their condition and discovering Jesus' healing power as they draw closer to him in prayer.

PRAYER

Thank you, Lord, for your promise to be with us always, to the end of the age. Thank you that when we are weak, you are strong; that when we are faithless, you are faithful; that when we are frightened, you renew our courage; and that when we are in chaos, you give us clarity. Thank you for the gift of prayer and the grace to believe that if we speak to you honestly, you will hear and respond. Be with us and with our addicted loved ones. Heal us all in your good time and in your good way, according to your perfect will and in your perfect wisdom and love. Amen.

Bibliography

Baker, John. "Pastor John's Testimony." (www.celebraterecovery.com)

Daniel, Orville E. *A Harmony of the Four Gospels, The New International Version*, 2nd ed. Grand Rapids, MI: Baker Books, 1996.

Keller, Timothy. "John Meets Jesus." New York: Redeemer Presbyterian Church Sermon CD, 4/27/97.

———. "Marriage in Christ." New York: Redeemer Presbyterian Church Sermon CD, 1/15/12.

Lewis, C. S. *The Great Divorce*. New York: Collier Books/Macmillan, 1946.

———. *Mere Christianity*. New York: Collier Books/Macmillan, 1960.

———. *Surprised by Joy: The Shape of My Early Life*. London: Collins, 1955.

The Life Recovery Bible: New Living Translation, 2nd ed. Carol Stream, IL: Tyndale House, 2007.

McClain, Joy. *Waiting for His Heart: Lessons from a Wife Who Chose to Stay*. Chicago: Moody Publishers, 2012.

Marshall, Catherine. *Light in My Darkest Night: The Unforgettable Testament of a Believer's Most Bitter Trial and Her Most Glorious Triumph*. New York: Avon, 1989.

————. *Something More: In Search of a Deeper Faith.* New York: McGraw-Hill, 1974.

May, Gerald. *Addiction and Grace: Love and Spirituality in the Healing of Addictions.* San Francisco: HarperSan-Francisco, 1988.

O'Connor, Elizabeth. *Journey Inward, Journey Outward.* New York: Harper & Row, 1968.

————. *Our Many Selves: A Handbook for Self-Discovery.* New York: Harper & Row, 1971.

Rohr, Richard. "Reflections on Marriage and Celibacy." *Sojourners* 8, no. 5 (May 1979).

About the Author

THE AUTHOR uses the pseudonym ALYSSA PHILLIPS to protect the privacy of family and friends in this collection of meditations on the challenges and gifts encountered in relationships with addicted loved ones. Under her given name she has written devotionals over the years that have appeared in various anthologies, and she has reviewed hundreds of books in the area of inspirational literature. She has a special interest in the intersections between psychology and faith and is the author of two previous books that explore some of these issues.

Alyssa, a graduate of Harvard University, holds a master's degree in Pastoral Ministry from the University of Saint Joseph. She has worked extensively with addicted men and women, serving as a volunteer through several church-based ministries. She lives with her husband in New England.